How to Find
Business Information

How to Find Business Information

A Guide for Businesspeople, Investors, and Researchers

Lucy Heckman

 PRAEGER

AN IMPRINT OF ABC-CLIO, LLC
Santa Barbara, California • Denver, Colorado • Oxford, England

Copyright 2011 by Lucy Heckman

Library of Congress Cataloging-in-Publication Data

Heckman, Lucy, 1954–
How to find business information : a guide for business people, investors, and researchers / Lucy Heckman.
    p. cm.
Includes bibliographical references and index.
ISBN 978–0–313–36280–4 (hardback : acid-free paper) — ISBN 978–0–313–36281–1 (ebook)
1. Business—Research. 2. Internet searching. I. Title.
HD30.4.H43   2011
016.65—dc23   2011024728

ISBN: 978–0–313–36280–4
EISBN: 978–0–313–36281–1

15 14 13 12   2 3 4 5

This book is also available on the World Wide Web as an eBook.
Visit www.abc-clio.com for details.

Praeger
An Imprint of ABC-CLIO, LLC

ABC-CLIO, LLC
130 Cremona Drive, P.O. Box 1911
Santa Barbara, California 93116-1911

This book is printed on acid-free paper ∞

Manufactured in the United States of America

Contents

Preface

Business and economics impacts our everyday lives in a variety of ways, from keeping track of the country's economic health to watching the securities markets to measuring the status of our portfolios to choosing our first home. Additionally, those studying business administration need resources to support their courses of study.

The Internet has led to the expansion and choice of more resources in additional formats; digital resources are updated more frequently and are essential to our decision making related to business and economics.

This book was written to help sort through the wide variety of material available digitally and in paper formats. Each chapter contains a brief introduction to its subject followed by an annotated listing of resources including encyclopedias and dictionaries, directories, data sources, guides, full-text periodical databases, periodicals and newspapers, government agencies, and trade associations.

The appendices contain a listing of acronyms and abbreviations and major business libraries; a directory of major business-related federal government departments, agencies, and resources; and a directory of major stock markets and security exchanges.

I would like to acknowledge the assistance in the preparation of this book, including St. John's University Library, St. John's University Tobin College of Business, New York Public Library's Science Industry and Business Library, Nassau Public Library System, and Queens Borough Public Library. Thanks also to my editor, Brian Romer, for his help and support.

Introduction: The Business Research Process—Guides to Guides and Resources to Build the Business Collection

INTRODUCTION

The world of business research has changed dramatically particularly over the past 15 years with the expansion of Internet resources. Websites available via the Internet have provided quick access to materials previously only accessible in print form, and in many cases, organizations, companies, and government agencies provide their resources only in digital formats. Additionally, over the past few years, ebooks have proliferated and publishers now have business monographs and serials available in both print and electronic formats. Examples of these include the *Advertising Red Books*, the *International Directory of Company Histories, Value Line Investment Survey,* Standard & Poor's publications, and Commerce Clearing House resources.

The changeover from print to electronic has significantly impacted research strategies. The availability of full-text periodical databases has made research more efficient but also has involved learning and using the best search strategies to locate these full-text articles.

A myriad of questions face both researchers and librarians regarding business information. How does the business researcher determine which are the best sources to use? How does a librarian who has a limited budget and building a collection determine the best business sources for company and industry research? How do both librarians and researchers keep up with the latest developments in resources for business research? How does the researcher keep up with the rapidly changing formats and publications some of which can become quickly outdated? In this guide, materials will be reviewed and appraised, and advice will be provided on how to select the most relevant materials to research in various fields. This source is designed for researchers and for both public and academic librarians, all of whom need to make choices and decisions on the best resources to select for collections and use for research by their patrons.

The public librarian must ensure that resources are available for the community including prospective entrepreneurs who want to start a business and need data and guides; investors looking for stock prices or market advice via *Value Line*; someone getting tax advice; and recent college graduates looking for a job who need to research company information. The academic librarian must work with the business school or faculty to make sure that materials are available to support the curricula, and reference librarians need to have materials to assist students in such projects as doing ratio analysis of companies and industries, finding a specific tax case, and writing a term paper about the current financial crisis.

This chapter addresses the research process and provides a list of recommended guides to guides to business information, which includes books, journals, and professional organizations, and how librarians can keep track of and select from the many new business sources out on the market in print and digital formats.

THE BUSINESS RESEARCH PROCESS

One of the ways to start the research process is to consult the guide to guides to business information. This series of guides by information professionals puts together and evaluates major sources related to specific topics in business. A researcher, for instance, can consult one of the guides and find a list of recommended resources and comparing and contrasting them. For instance, if a researcher wants the major guides in finance, he would find lists of annotated materials ranging from *Value Line* to the New York Stock Exchange's website.

GUIDE TO GUIDES

The business research process may begin for some with the examination of materials available on each subject and explanations on how to use them. The guides-to-guides reference books provide an overview on the research process and discuss how to use specific resources and offer advice on the ones to select. Over the past few decades, there have been key guides to the use of business literature—a pioneer in this effort was Lorna M. Daniells, former business bibliographer at Harvard University's Baker Library. She wrote three editions of *Business Information Sources*, the last in 1993, an annotated guide to major business sources and a source consulted by reference librarians and library and information science students.

Following Daniells's various editions, other business guides by subject specialists included Michael Lavin's *Business Information: How to Find it, How to Use It* and Ruth Pagell's *International Business Information: How to Find It, How to Use It*.

The following are some representative guides to business research and information. Some sources listed are outdated, but these books have set the standard for future guides. Additionally, core materials are listed. Advice on how to select materials for research and the research process itself really does not change. Some materials are "classics" in the field, notably the works by Daniells, Lavin, and Pagell.

The following are introductory guides to business research and resources:

The Basic Business Library: Core Resources. 4th ed. Edited by Rashelle S. Karp with Bernard S. Schlessinger, associate editor. Westport, CT: Greenwood Press, 2002.

According to its editors, *the Basic Business Library* is a "checklist of essential business reference tools that smaller libraries can use to evaluate their business reference collections and services, and as a core list and set of essays for smaller libraries beginning a business reference area. . . . An additional objective, recognized after the third edition began to be used as a text for library science courses, is to serve the needs of library science professors and their students." The fourth edition includes Internet sources and digitized formats. This source contains a core list and bibliographic essays on business libraries: changing collections, services, and roles; business databases, U.S. government information sources for business; business periodicals; the best investment sources, acquisitions, and collection development in business; practice of organization in business libraries and information centers; reference in the business area; and marketing the business library. Each source contains bibliographic information, including cost and analysis of "authority and scope" and "evaluation."

Daniells, Lorna. *Business Information Sources*. 3rd ed. Berkeley: University of California Press, 1993.

According to its author, the book "is intended as a guide to the vast and varied sources of business information for three types of users: 1) the practicing business person . . . 2) the business student . . .; and 3. the librarian and information specialist." Daniells covers research methods and a guide to sources (online and print) representing management, marketing, accounting/control and taxation, finance and investment, economics, insurance and real estate, and computers and information management systems. Her chapter "A Basic Bookshelf" is a guide to essential sources for the business library. Daniell not only covers reference materials but also reviews and annotates key journals, monographs, and textbooks with attention to seminal works such as Malkiel's *A Random Walk down Wall Street* and management books by Peter Drucker.

Lavin, Michael R. *Business Information: How to Find It, How to Use It.* 2nd ed. Phoenix, AZ: Oryx Press, 1992.

Lavin provides "in depth descriptions of major business publications and databases." The guide is designed for both beginners to advanced researchers and is designed for those in graduate library schools to businesspeople, students, and researchers. Sources examined include guides to business literature and sources of company information, finance and investments, banking, industry statistics, census information, economic statistics, marketing, business law, and taxation and accounting. Chapters contain bibliographies for further reading (e.g., articles about research methods in specific areas of business). It also includes sample pages of key material among which are Predicasts, *Standard & Poor's Register of Corporations,* and *Census of Manufacturers.*

Moss, Rita W. *Strauss's Handbook of Business Information: A Guide for Librarians, Students, and Researchers.* 2nd ed. Westport, CT: Libraries Unlimited, 2004.

This is a revised edition of Diane Wheeler Strauss's *Handbook of Business Information* (1988). The handbook is divided into two parts: the first covers business information sources in specific formats (guides, bibliographies, directories, and quick reference sources), and the second focuses on specific topics within the area of business. Subjects related to business covered are marketing, accounting and taxation, real estate, insurance, finance and investments, banking, and statistics.

Pagell, Ruth A., and Michael Halperin. *International Business Information: How to Find It, How to Use It.* Phoenix, AZ: Oryx Press, 1998.

Pagell and Halperin focus on sources for international business research, including general sources, company information, marketing, industrial and economic statistics, exporting and importing, and international transactions. Covered are print and digital materials and websites. Each chapter presents subject background first and then coverage of the information sources related to that subject. Illustrations from selected publications are included. It is intended for the researcher, ranging from beginner to advanced.

RESOURCES TO BUILD THE BUSINESS COLLECTION AND KEEPING UP TO DATE

Collection development and research involves keeping current. While business guides can give a background to research methods and introduce "core" materials, there are always new products on the market or revisions to current resources. Keeping up with the literature is an ongoing process. For example, the financial crisis of 2008 created a plethora of new books and articles related to this topic. Also, formats are continuously updated, and there have been mergers among publishers and vendors of needed materials.

To analyze these items and keep up to date, the following strategies are recommended:

In an academic setting, the business librarian reviews the syllabi and selects items to support courses in the business program. A Library Committee or Learning Resources Committee consisting of representatives from both the library and the business school facilitates the selection of materials. If there is no committee in the business school, the library business subject specialist has the option to appear at faculty council meetings, have office hours in the business school, or be on call by faculty for advisement and discussion about new sources. Additionally, the business librarian or collection development librarian could present in-house demonstrations of new products and invite the business faculty. Requesting current syllabi from the faculty/administrators of the business school is highly recommended to ensure that the library has the resources to support research of students and faculty.

In the public library setting, the business librarian examines research needs of the population it serves—selecting materials for both central and branch libraries. Generally, the public librarian business specialist would consider books about starting up a small business, books about buying a home, personal finance guides, income tax–related how-to sources, and finance and investment guides (which stocks to buy or sell). Public librarians also may sponsor special "clinics" of how to start a small business or how to work on income taxes for the community, including a display or handouts of recommended titles.

Both academic and public librarians are advised to use current awareness materials to advise them and inform them about new books/databases on the market.

The following materials are recommended:

American Reference Books Annual (ARBA) (http://www.arbaonline.com). Santa
Barbara, CA: Libraries Unlimited. Annual. Print and online.
   Features reviews of the year's reference sources, print and online; topics
   covered include business and economics. Reviews highlight content of
   source and compares and contrasts (when applicable) with other titles
   that cover similar subject areas. A good annual checklist for business
   librarians updating a collection.

Choice (Choice Reviews Online) (http://www.cro2.org). Chicago: Association
of College and Research Libraries, American Library Association.
   Primarily for academic librarians, but business librarians from all types of
   libraries should benefit by consulting this monthly journal, in print and
   online versions. In addition to the book reviews, *Choice* features bibliographical essays on a variety of topics. Reviews contain all bibliographic
   components including ISBN and prices.

Harvard University. New Books in Baker Library/Bloomberg Center (http://
www.library.hbs.edu/bakerbooks/recent).
   A monthly list of books acquired by the Baker Library. Contains alphabetical list of new books with bibliographic citations. Citations do not include
   prices or ISBNs.

Journal of Business and Finance Librarianship, vol. 1, 1990. New York: Routledge.
   Quarterly, print and online.
   The *Journal of Business & Finance Librarianship* is a refereed journal for special, academic, and public libraries that is international in scope and
   focuses on business information and its "creation, organization, dissemi-
   nation, retrieval, and use." The journal provides reviews and analyses
   of new books and major databases in business as well as websites. This
   journal provides in-depth analysis and scholarly articles on trends in business information, research methods, and resources representing various
   areas of business.

Library Journal. Semimonthly except in January, July, August, and December.
   New York: Library Journals, LLC, a wholly owned subsidiary of Media
   Source, Inc. (http://www.libraryjournal.com). Print and online.
   Each issue features book reviews in economics (including finance, management, and marketing) and a prepub alert featuring selected business
   books. There is an annual Best Business Books of the Year section (published every March). Additionally contains articles on best books and online resources for specific topics—past issues have included focus on
   resources for specific topics (e.g., the financial crisis of 2008–2009). The
   reviews and books examined in essays and prepub alert contain all bibliographic information, including ISBN and prices.

Publishers Weekly. New York: PWxyz, LLC, 1872–
   (http://www.publishersweekly.com/pw/home/index.html).

In addition to news of the publishing trade and its trends, this journal focuses on new books and announcements of forthcoming books and contains best-seller lists. Good source for ratings of new books plus valuable announcements of new publications.

ASSOCIATIONS

In addition to the print/digital guides, there are several recommended organizations. Librarians can become members and participate in the various subcommittees and attend seminars related to specific business research topics.

American Library Association. Business Reference and Services Section (BRASS). American Library Association, 50 East Huron Street, Chicago IL 60611; 1-800-545-2433 (http://www.ala.org).
A section of the ALA's Reference and User Services Association (RUSA), BRASS is an organization specializing in business reference sources and services, and members are from various types of libraries, including academic, public, and corporate. Among the committees of BRASS are Business Reference in Public Libraries, Business Reference in Academic Libraries, Business Reference Sources, Business Reference Services Discussion Group, Vendor Relations Committee, Publications, Program Planning, and Publications. BRASS sponsors preconference seminars and an annual program on a specific topic in business and sources for research on this topic. Past annual programs have covered, among other topics, green business, accounting, business law, and global business.

Special Libraries Association (SLA), 331 South Patrick Street, Alexandria, VA 22314-3501; 703-647-4900 (http://www.sla.org).
Among its divisions is Business and Finance, with members representing various types of libraries: special, academic, and public. The annual conference features meetings on specific topics in business, vendor presentations, continuing education seminars, and exhibits. SLA also has regional divisions representing various areas of the United States.

CONSULTATION WITH INFORMATION PROFESSIONALS (SEE APPENDIX II, "MAJOR BUSINESS LIBRARIES")

A business researcher's questions could include "quick reference" questions, such as what is the ticker symbol for General Motors; the latest evaluation by *Value Line* of Apple Computer; and the current chief executive officer of Alitalia. In-depth questions could include the annual advertising expenses for 20 years for General Motors, the reasons why the Securities and Exchange Act of 1934 was passed, and locating business ratios for two industries (for the past 10 years).

The business librarian/information professional is a key source of research assistance. The librarian/information professional would first have a reference interview with the patron to discuss research strategies, specific question(s) that are needed to be addressed, and recommendation of sources. Instruction in the use of digital materials may also be a part of the research process.

Public libraries, including the New York Public Library's Science, Industry, and Business Library, offers one-on-one consultation and offers classes and seminars related to specific issues in business as well as research guides.

Academic libraries supporting business curricula offer research assistance; some librarians have office hours in the college/university's business school to assist faculty and students.

The addition of electronic reference in both types of libraries allows patrons to email or text questions to business specialists for research help.

Many university and public libraries include print and online bibliographies and research guides. Some of the sources would not be "free" to those who are not affiliated with a university or public library, but it should be noted that these guides often contain "free" access to websites containing information. For instance, St. John's University Library contains a Business Subject guide that groups by specific topics in business and does include a list of related "free" websites.

2

How to Find Industry Information

Researching industries is frequently the subject of assignments by students of business, business school faculty, and patrons exploring possible stock and bond purchases by examining industries. Questions range from comparing the top five companies in the automobile industry, identifying the rising stars of retailers, finding industry ratios, and locating North American Industry Classification System (NAICS) and Standard Industrial Classification (SIC) codes. This chapter will address how to locate the various aspects of industry research.

LOCATING NAICS AND SIC CODES

How can I find the NAICS and SIC code for a specific company? This is a very frequent request that is heard at reference desks, particularly those in academic libraries where students are assigned a research paper. What are these codes? The first step in industry research is often first locating the SIC or the NAICS code or both.

The Standard Industrial Classification

The Standard Industrial Classification (SIC) code was prepared by the Office of Management and Budget. According to the preface of the code, it "is the statistical classification standard underlying all establishment-based Federal economic statistics classified by industry." Divisions of the SIC Code are A. Agricultural, Forestry, and Fishing; B. Mining; C. Construction; D. Manufacturing; E. Transportation,

Communications, Electric, Gas, and Sanitary Services; F. Wholesale Trade; G. Retail Trade; H. Finance, Insurance and Real Estate; I. Services; and J. Public Administration.

Within each division, there is a further breakdown from general to most specific. For instance, to locate SIC codes for the Airline Industry, first go to Division E. Transportation, Communications, Electric, Gas, and Sanitary Services, then select Major group 45 within this category—Transportation by Air—to locate the following subcategories:

45. Transportation by Air
   451 Air Transportation, Scheduled and Air Courier Services
      4512 Air Transportation, Scheduled
      4513 Air Courier Services
   452 Air Transportation, Nonscheduled
      4522 Air Transportation, Nonscheduled
   458 Airports, Flying Fields and Airport Terminal Services

Within each division and categories, there is an explanation of the specific industry category. In some cases, a company can have multiple industry categories and be assigned several SIC codes.

The NAICS was designed to replace the SIC code. However, some government sources, including the Securities and Exchange Commission, and commercial publishers still use the SIC codes along with NAICS.

Sources for Locating SIC Codes

Standard Industrial Classification Manual 1987, by United States Office of Management and Budget. Washington, DC: The Office (Superintendent of Documents, U.S. Government Printing Office, distributor). Springfield, VA: For Sale by the National Technical Information Service, 1987.

U.S. Department of Labor, Occupational Safety and Health Administration (OSHA). *SIC Division Structure* (http://www.osha.gov/pls/imis/sicsearch.html)
   Searchable database by code and by industry with structure of SIC Divisions and Industry groups.

The North American Industry Classification System

The North American Industry Classification System (NAICS), implemented in 1997, is, according to the preface of its 2007 edition, "constructed within a single conceptual framework. Economic units that have similar production processes are classified in the same industry." It uses a six-digit hierarchical coding system to classify all economic activity into 20 industry sectors with industries in these sectors grouped "according to the production criteria." The NAICS was developed under the auspices of the Office of Management and Budget, officially adopted in 1997, and "developed jointly by the U.S. Economic Classification Policy Committee (ECPC), Statistics Canada, and Mexico's Instituto Nacional de Estadistica y Geografia, to allow for a high level of comparability in business statistics among the North American countries" (U.S. Census website, http://www.census.gov/eos/www/naics). The latest edition of the NAICS code is the 2007 edition.

The sectors of the NAICS are 11. Agriculture, Forestry, Fishing, and Hunting; 21. Mining, Quarrying, and Oil and Gas Extraction; 22. Utilities; 23. Construction; 31–33. Manufacturing; 42. Wholesale Trade; 44–45. Retail Trade; 48–49. Transportation and Warehousing; 51. Information (including publishing, motion pictures, broadcasting, telecommunications, data processing, online information services); 52. Finance and Insurance; 53. Real Estate and Rental and Leasing; 54. Professional, Scientific and Technical Services; 55. Management of Companies and Enterprises; 56. Administrative and Support and Waste Management and Remediation Services; 61. Educational Services; 62. Health Care and Social Assistance; 71. Arts, Entertainment and Recreation; 72. Accommodation and Food Service; 81. Other Services (except Public Administration); and 92. Public Administration.

As with the SIC, the individual categories go from general to more specific. The Airline Industry in NAICS is categorized as follows:

Section 48–49 Transportation and Warehousing
    Section 481 Air Transportation
        4811 Scheduled Air Transportation 481111 Scheduled Passenger Air
        Transportation 481112 Scheduled Freight Air Transportation

It should be noted that many sources provide both NAICS and SIC codes, including U.S. government websites and commercial publications.

Sources for Locating NAICS Codes

North American Industry Classification System: United States 2007, by United States Executive Office of the President, United States, Office of Management and Budget. Lanham, MD: Bernan; Springfield, VA. National Technical Information Service, 2007.

North American Industry Classification System: United States 2002, by United States Executive Office of the President, United States, Office of Management and Budget. Lanham, MD: Bernan; Springfield, VA: National Technical Information Service, 2002.

North American Industry Classification System: United States 1997, by United
    States Office of the President, Office of the President, United States.
    Washington, DC: Executive Office of the President, Office of Management
    and Budget, U.S. Government Printing Office, 1997.
U.S. Census Bureau. North American Industry Classification System (http://
    www.census.gov/eos/www/naics).
U.S. Department of Labor. North American Industry Classification System
    (http://www.osha.gov/oshstats/naics-manual.html).

LOCATING INDUSTRY DATA FROM COMMERCIAL PUBLISHERS

To locate current reports about how a specific industry is performing,
what are the trends, and what are future projections, several publications offer current information, among which are the publishers
Hoover's, Mergent, and Standard & Poor's. The following are "staples"
in locating specific industry reports.

Hoover's (http://www.hoovers.com).
    To locate industry information, select the "Industries" tab on the home
    page. Hoover's covers over 600 industries, and researchers use the search
    option or browse. The database arranges industries into browseable lists
    by general categories and then subcategories. General categories are aero-
    space and defense, agriculture, automotive and transportation, banking,
    beverage, business services, charitable organizations, chemicals, com-
    puter hardware, computer services, computer software, construction,
    consumer products manufacturers, consumer services, cultural organiza-
    tions, education, electronics, energy and utilities, environmental services
    and equipment, financial services, food, foundations, government, health
    care, industrial manufacturing, insurance, leisure, media, pharmaceuti-
    cals, real estate, retail, security products and services, telecommunica-
    tions equipment, telecommunications services, and transportation
    services. Each report provides SIC and NAICS code industry overviews;
    competitive landscapes; products, operations, and technology; and sales
    and marketing. Hoover's also offers the option for users to purchase com-
    plete online First Research Industry Profiles. Hoover's also publishes in
    print the following:

    Handbook of Industry Profiles: Analysis and Trends for 300 Industries. Austin,
    TX: Hoover's. Annual.

    Provides a comparative overview, sales and marketing processes, employ-
    ment trends and average wages, and so on.

Mergent. Industry Reports (http://www.mergent.com).
    To search for Mergent's industry reports, select the "report search" tab,
    then select "Industry Reports" to find a searchable list of industries. Mer-
    gent organizes the industry reports by regions: North America, Latin
    America, Europe, and Asia Pacific. Industries covered are automotive,

aviation, banking, biotechnology, chemicals, construction, construction—public infrastructure, consumer services, electricity, energy, food and beverage, health, health care, heavy construction, hospitality and tourism, hospitals and health care, insurance information technologies and communication, IT and high technology, media, medical instruments and equipment, mining, metal works, nonrecious metals, oil and gas, precious metals, pharmaceuticals, property and development, retail, retail-general, telecommunications, and textiles. Current and back issue reports are available in HTML or in Adobe Acrobat format. Each report contains overview of current industry trends; financial data, including sales; narrative analysis of the leading companies; market trends and outlook; and key references used in the report.

MERGENT

Automotive : North America

CURRENT ENVIRONMENT—UNITED STATES

Current Environment—Canada Industry Profile—Canada Industry Profile—US Key Points Key References Market Trends & Outlook US Market Trends & Outlook Canada Scope of this report

SECTOR OVERVIEW

The US automotive industry heaved a sigh of relief at the beginning of 2010 as they put the worst year for new car and truck sales in more than two decades behind them. In 2009, US car and truck sales took a steep dive, selling 10.6 million units in the midst of recession. It was a level not seen since 1982. A closer look revealed that all was not lost, however. The Bureau of Economic Analysis (BEA) estimates real GDP increased by 5.2% in the fourth quarter of 2009, after 3% growth in the previous quarter. Motor vehicle output added 0.45 of a percentage point to the fourth quarter change in real GDP after adding 1.45 percentage points to the third quarter change. With the economy improving, there was light at the other end of the tunnel. Dealers and automakers became optimistic that more consumers would be ready and able to replace their tired old wheels with a shiny new model.

The year 2009 was a watershed year, especially for Detroit's Big Three, as sweeping, major changes reshaped the US automotive sector. Automakers shuttered plants, cut jobs, reduced dealerships, renegotiated workers' wages and benefits, and dropped unprofitable models. After months of living on government loans, Chrysler sought bankruptcy protection on April 30, while GM filed for bankruptcy on June 1.

In just six weeks, on July 10 GM resurfaced as a new, leaner company that was 60% owned by the US Treasury—a much sooner recovery than expected. It shed 2,400 US dealerships and announced its intention to sell its Saturn, Saab, and Hummer brands, and phase out the Pontiac line. Chrysler exited bankruptcy on June 11, after it finalized its deal with Italian automaker Fiat (ITL: F), which owned 20% of the new company, and which will help Chrysler build smaller cars. In return, the Federal Government agreed to give Chrysler up to US$8 billion in additional aid and to back its warranties.

Although Ford (NYSE: F) has endured years of losses, it was in a better financial state than its peers, with enough cash on hand to finance its day-to-day operating needs until some time in 2010. It hoped that by then the market would have started to pick up. Nonetheless, it did make a request for a credit line of US$9 billion to support the development of a new eco-friendly product line-up. It is hard to remain upbeat, however, as the Big Three continue to address their strategic priorities, primarily to step up restructuring and other cost reduction efforts through staff lay-offs and discretionary spending.

The US auto industry turned a corner in the second half of 2009 when the US drew up its own stimulus program to soften the impact of the recession and at the same time promote greener cars. Various governments in Europe had already stepped in to help their beleaguered auto industries as early as the beginning of 2009, with the results positive. Major economies such as France, Germany and the UK introduced scrappage schemes to boost demand for new cars, giving car owners subsidies if they traded in their old cars for new, more fuel-efficient models.

In Asia, governments also studied ways of stimulating the market, including proposing different funding possibilities for the auto industry in Japan, and considering cutting commercial vehicle excise duties to counter rapidly shrinking sales in India. The Chinese Government pledged its support for the industry by subsidizing fuel prices and cutting car purchase taxes by half. The US version was called the Car Allowance Rebate System (CARS). The program began offering car owners a trade-in credit of between US$3,000 and US$4,500 for their old gas-guzzlers in exchange for new, more fuel-efficient models in July 2009.

Due to a rush in consumer demand, the Government added another US$2 billion when the initial US$1 billion appropriated for the program, otherwise known as "Cash for Clunkers," quickly ran out. The program was a success, making July and August the best months for auto sales in the past year. Although showroom traffic noticeably slowed after the program ended on August 24, the industry gained positive momentum for a gradual recovery and auto sales ended the year with an up tick.

Emerging from a rollercoaster year in 2009, the industry's seasonally adjusted annual rate in January 2010 was estimated to be approximately 11 million to 11.3 million of new car sales, largely on par with 2009's fourth quarter sales. With sales picking up, auto dealers received offers to be reinstated. GM was prepared to restore 660 of its 2,000 terminated dealers while Chrysler offered up to 86 dealers a chance to seek reinstatement. Under its reorganization plan, Chrysler eliminated a quarter of its US dealerships in 2009.

US Vehicle Sales (in units)

		Year-to-Date		
		January–March	Volume	
	Year 2009	2010	2009	% Change
Domestic cars	n/a	907,085	709,124	27.9
Imported cars	n/a	394,862	392,486	0.6
Total cars	5.456 million	1,301,947	1,101,610	18.2
Domestic light trucks	n/a	1,030,625	864,993	19.1
Imported light trucks	n/a	206,280	230,442	−10.5
Total light trucks	5.145 million	1,236,905	1,095,435	12.9
Total light vehicles	**10.601 million**	**2,538,852**	**2,197,045**	**15.6**

Source: Wards Auto
Note: n/a denotes not available

SECTOR PERFORMANCE

During the second half of 2009, the Dow Jones Industrial Average (DJIA) picked up steadily as the Government's stimulus injection of US$787 billion started to make an impact, albeit sluggishly. Since July 1, 2009, DJIA had been on an upward trend, registering an increase of 28% at 10.428 at the end of the year. While unemployment rates remained elevated, consumer confidence and business sentiments improved. The Dow Jones US Auto & Parts (DJUSAT) Index, which tracks 16 auto companies, recorded an even more impressive gain of 32.4% between July and December 2009.

Although GM and Chrysler filed for Chapter 11 bankruptcy the first half of the year, the market regarded this as a positive change. Meanwhile, Ford ended the year with an outstanding stock performance. As the automaker's viability improved after significant restructuring and buoyant sales, Ford's shares soared from the year's low of US$1.58 in February 2009 to a historical high of US$10.00 in December 2009.

Asian automakers trading on the New York Stock Exchange also emerged from the financial crisis. After double-digit falls in their US shares in 2008, Toyota (TSE: 7203) and Honda (TSE: 7267) registered healthy growth following announcements that they would produce zero emission vehicles. In 2009, Toyota's shares on the NYSE rose 12.48% over the six months ended December 31, 2009. Honda added 28.9% to its value in the US over the six-month period.

LEADING AUTOMAKERS

General Motors

On July 10, a new GM was born. The slimmed down GM was still the largest automaker in US, with a 19.58% market share, but the gap was closing in, with Toyota (16.73%) and Ford (15.29%) hot on its wheels. As part of a revised viability plan, and with the need to move faster and further, the new company cut the number of brands from eight to four, retaining Chevrolet, Cadillac, Buick and GMC. At least 14 facilities, including assembly lines in Pontiac, Michigan and Wilmington, Delaware, and three parts distribution warehouses, were identified for closure. Three plants, including assembly lines in Spring Hill, Tennessee, and Orion, Michigan, were planned to be idled and were put on stand-by status waiting for a rebound in sales. . . .

Excerpt of Sample Industry Report From Mergent Online, Automobile Reports, North America, April 2010 issue, used with permission of Mergent.

Standard & Poor's NetAdvantage. Industry Surveys (http://www.netadvantage
.standardandpoors.com/NASApp/NetAdvantage/servlet/login?url=/
NASApp/NetAdvantage/index.do)
  Researchers can access the "Industries" section on the tab of the database home page and then either search or browse "Industry Surveys" to locate a selection of industry reports by searching or browsing through the list. Select the "Industry Surveys" link to locate the list of reports and browse or search by company name or its ticker symbol to find the industry of that company. Industry Survey reports cover advertising; aerospace and defense; agribusiness; airlines; alcoholic beverages and tobacco; apparel and footwear; autos and auto parts; banking; biotechnology; broadcasting

and cable; chemicals; chemicals: specialty; communications equipment; computers, storage and peripherals; computers: commercial services; computers: consumer services and the internet; computers: hardware; computers: networking; computers: software; electric utilities; environmental and waste management; financial services: diversified; foods and nonalcoholic beverages; health care; facilities; healthcare: managed care; healthcare: pharmaceuticals; healthcare: products and supplies; heavy equipment and trucks; home building; household durables; household nondurables; industrial machinery; insurance: life and health; insurance: property/casualty; investment services; lodging and gaming; metals: industrial; metals: precious; moving and home entertainment: natural gas: distribution; oil and gas: equipment and services; oil and gas: production and marketing; paper and forest products; publishing: REITS; restaurants: general; retailing; general; retailing: specialty; savings and loans; semiconductor equipment; semiconductors: supermarkets and drugstores; telecommunications: wireless; telecommunications: wireline; and transportation: commercial. Industry surveys are accessible in both PDF and HTML formats and include current and back issues generally encompassing the past 12 years. Each report provides a description of the current industry environment (new developments and possible mergers), key industry ratios, comparative company analysis, industry trends, and a list of resources (websites and trade journals) related to that specific industry.

STANDARD & POOR'S NET ADVANTAGE

STANDARD & POOR'S
INDUSTRY
SURVEYS

Airlines

June 17, 2010
Jim Corridore
Airlines & Air Freight Analyst

CURRENT ENVIRONMENT   **INDUSTRY REFERENCES**
INDUSTRY PROFILE
Industry Trends   **COMPARATIVE COMPANY ANALYSIS**
How the Industry Operates   Revenues Net Income Profit Ratios
Key Industry Ratios and Statistics Balance Sheet Ratios Equity Ratios Per-Share Data
How to Analyze an Airline

CURRENT ENVIRONMENT

United-Continental Merger Would Surpass Delta as World's Largest Airline

On May 3, 2010, UAL Corp., parent of United Airlines, and Continental Airlines Inc. announced that they intend to merge, creating a global airline with combined 2009 revenues of $29 billion. Standard & Poor's

believes the combined carrier would become the largest passenger airline in the world in terms of passenger revenues. Under terms of the
deal, United would be the acquirer, with each Continental share getting
1.05 UAL shares. A new holding company would be formed, called
United Continental Holdings Inc. The company would fly under the
United name, but would use Continental's logo, livery, and colors. The
new company's headquarters would be in Chicago, United's headquarters, but Houston, Continental's main hub, would remain the combined company's largest hub. The companies hoped to complete the
merger by the end of the fourth quarter of 2010.

Standard & Poor's thinks the deal makes strategic sense because
there is not much overlap between the carriers. Internationally, United
has a strong market presence in Europe and flies out of hubs that
include Chicago and Los Angeles, while Continental flies internationally out of its hubs at Newark's Liberty International Airport and Houston. For this reason, we think the two airlines will complement each
other in getting passengers to and from Europe. Continental would also
add its strong Latin America network to the combination, while United
has strength in the Pacific region, including China. The companies say
they do not plan to cut any hubs or eliminate any markets after the
merger closes. We think the combined carrier would be a truly global
airline, allowing its passengers to travel throughout the world.

Getting approval by regulatory authorities may be difficult due to
the sheer size of the combined carrier, but Standard & Poor's thinks that
since there's so little overlap between the two airlines, a case could be
made that this merger is not at all anticompetitive. In addition, the companies' stated intention not to close any markets or hubs should work in
their favor (though it would reduce the merger's potential cost savings).
In fact, Continental and United customers will each gain many more
travel choices throughout the world.

As to the composition of the fleet, both carriers primarily fly Boeing
planes, which should help keep expense items like training, maintenance,
and spare parts from becoming an issue. With several kinds of Boeing jets
in use, the companies should be able to put the right-sized airplane into
the right market, driving revenue synergy opportunities. The deal would
also give the combined airline flexibility in streamlining the fleet and eliminating older, less fuel–efficient planes. Even before any such elimination,
the combined carrier is expected to have an average aircraft age of
11.5 years, still among the youngest in the industry. The companies said
that over the next few years, they could fly as few as 550 to as many as
700 planes, depending on industry conditions, which we think should
afford them remarkable opportunities to capitalize on improving demand,
with the ability to scale back if the industry does not recover.

The companies said cost synergies are targeted at $1.2 billion, which
we think is a conservative estimate and achievable. Savings are targeted
by eliminating redundancies in reservations, ticketing, and other back-
office functions. Labor is likely to add costs, as we think the unionized

employees will be brought up to the higher of the two contracts. However, the $1.2 billion cost savings target stated by the companies is net of any expected additional costs resulting from labor contracts.

From Standard & Poor's NetAdvantage, Industry Surveys, Airline Industry Report, June 17, 2010. Used with Permission of Standard & Poor's.

U.S. GOVERNMENT—ECONOMIC CENSUS

U.S. Census (http://factfinder.census.gov/servlet/DatasetMainPageServlet?
_program=ECN&_submenuId=datasets_4&_lang=en&_ts=)
On the U.S. Census page, business and industry data are accessible. The Economic Census is issued every five years (years ending in a 2 or a 7) The Census determines how many business establishments there are within specific industries. Within the category "Business and Government," there are two links applicable to industry data: "Economic Fact Sheet" and "Business and Industry." The "Economic Fact Sheet" yields selected statistics from the 2007 Census—listing industries' number of establishment; sales, shipments, and receipts; annual payroll; and number of employees. "Economic Fact Sheet" allows searching of more specific products/services—for instance, it provides data for dog and cat food manufacturing from the 2007 Economic Census. "Business and Industry" allows searching by state and city/town—many of the data are from 2008. Data are searchable by NAICS codes. For more information, consult "About the Economic Census" at http://www.census.gov/econ/census07/.

LOCATING INDUSTRY INFORMATION FROM JOURNAL
AND NEWSPAPER ARTICLES

Obtaining the most current industry information is frequently of prime importance to a researcher. Keeping up with industry developments requires searching online databases to locate needed data. Of special value are the materials found in trade journals (e.g., covering the airline industry) that often feature "special issues or reports" on the state of the industry.

ABI/INFORM (ProQuest) (http://www.proquest.com/en-US/catalogs/databases/detail/abi_inform.shtml).
ProQuest is a part of Cambridge Information Group (CSA) (http://www.cambridgeinformationgroup.com). *ABI/INFORM* is also available through Dialog.

Coverage includes journal articles some going back as far as 1923. Full text is included for many of the articles added from 1991 to present. Provides related topics for searchers and enables users to select full text only or scholarly only (excluding popular titles). The *ABI/INFORM* product line includes *ABI/INFORM Complete, ABI/INFORM Global, ABI/INFORM Research, ABI/INFORM Select, ABI/INFORM Trade and Industry,* and *ABI/ INFORM Dateline:*

ABI/INFORM Complete—Covers over 5,400 journals, nearly 80 percent of which are in full text. Includes complete industry research reports from Business Monitor International (BMI).

ABI/INFORM Dateline—Focus is on regional and local publications; covers 190 journals with 170 in full text.

ABI/INFORM Global—Covers over 3,000 publications.

ABI/INFORM Research—Covers over 1,800 journals, 1,100 in full text.

ABI/INFORM Select—Concentration on business news; covers over 500 journals, 400 in full text.

ABI/INFORM Trade and Industry—Focus is on trade and industry news reports; concentrates on trade publications. Covers over 2,000 publications.

Business Periodicals Index (H. W. Wilson) (http://www.hwwilson.com/ databases/business_retro.cfm and http://www.hwwilson.com/databases/ business.cfm).

Business Periodicals Index, available in print and online formats, provides indexing only to articles in business and economics. *Business Periodicals Index Retrospective* provides indexing of articles from 1913 to 1982. H. W. Wilson also offers for sale selected back volumes of print issues of *Business Periodicals Index.*

Business Source Complete (*EBSCOhost*) (http://www.ebscohost.com/thisTopic .php?marketID=1&topicID=399).

Indexes and abstracts of scholarly articles, books, faculty seminars (videos), industry reports, scholarly journals, trade journals, market research reports, and monographs, among other resources. Features profiles of the most-cited authors of articles.

Business Source Elite (*EBSCOhost*) (http://www.ebscohost.com/thisTopic.php ?topicID=4&marketID=1).

Provides full-text coverage of approximately 1,000 scholarly journals in business, economics, and management. Also features company profiles from Datamonitor.

Business Source Premier (*EBSCOhost*) (http://www.ebscohost.com/thisTopic .php?topicID=2&marketID=1).

Full-text coverage is available for over 2,300 journals. Searches can be limited to full text and/or scholarly journals (peer reviewed) only. The Business Searching Interface enables researchers to locate full-text industry profiles and trade journals. International in focus, these industry reports are from Datamonitor plc.

Dow Jones Factiva (http://factiva.com).

Searchable database of over 14,000 leading news and business sources, among which are over 60 newswires, over 2,500 newspapers, over 5,500

business and industry publications, selected television and radio transcripts, and pictures from wire services, among which are Reuters and
McClatchy-Tribune Photo Service.

Journal Storage (JSTOR) (http://www.jstor.org).
Multidisciplinary database provides extensive back file of full-text journal
articles. Those researching business can browse related journals divided
into categories of business, economics, and finance or search by topic
for full-text articles. Enables company researchers to locate historical
articles about companies.

Regional Business News (EBSCOhost) (http://www.ebscohost.com/thisTopic
.php?marketID=1&topicID=130).
Contains full-text coverage of approximately 80 local business publications
from the United States and Canada—good search tool for local or small or
smaller companies. Academic Library subscribers to Business Source Premier, Business Source Elite, or Business Source Complete receive access
to Regional Business News.

ScienceDirect (http://www.sciencedirect.com).
A scholarly journals focus, coverage includes full-text articles in economics, econometrics and finance and business, management, and accounting. Contains scholarly articles and features "search alerts" and allows
searching by affiliation of authors.

Wall Street Journal (http://online.wsj.com/home-page).
The *Wall Street Journal* is a prime current awareness source about industries and companies. It is available online from the publisher but also
via vendors, including ProQuest which offers both full-text coverage of
current issues and back files.

Wilson Business Abstracts (http://www.hwwilson.com/databases/business.cfm).
Features only indexing and abstracting of articles from over 400 publications,
including popular magazines and full text, but does not provide full text.

Wilson Business Full Text (H. W. Wilson) (http://www.hwwilson.com/databases/
business.cfm).
Provides full text articles from over 500 publications, including popular
magazines and scholarly journals.. Subscribers can also opt to purchase
Wilson Business Abstracts.

ENCYCLOPEDIA

Historical Encyclopedia of American Business. Edited by Richard L. Wilson. Pasa-
dena, CA: Salem Press, 2009. 3 volumes.
Covers the "breadth of American business history" and covers topics
related to companies, industries, individuals, organizations, and legislation. Among articles are entries about industries in historical context—
with bibliographic references and cross-references.

THE INDUSTRY TRADE ASSOCIATION AS A SOURCE OF INDUSTRY RESEARCH

At times a researcher may look through the commercial publications, government materials, articles and still not find the needed data for a project. To locate additional, needed material, finding the trade association is the next step.

Industries have trade associations which are generally consisting of representatives from various industries as members. Trade associations often publish key industry journals, newspapers, and newsletters which researchers may want to consult.

Encyclopedia of Associations (Print and Online)

Gale Directory Library.
> Searchable database provides access to Gale publications, including the *Encyclopedia of Associations*—international, national, regional, state, and local. For instance, searching "automobile" yields a list of trade associations, among which are the American Automobile Association and the National Automobile Dealers Association. Additional data about an aspect of an industry researched may be obtained by checking the company website and/or contacting the association for additional material. Encyclopedias of associations are also available in print editions:
>
> *Encyclopedia of Associations.* Detroit: Gale Research, 1961–.
> *Encyclopedia of Associations: International Organizations.* Detroit: Gale Research, 1989–.
> *Encyclopedia of Associations: Regional, State, and Local Organizations.* Detroit: Gale Research, 1987–.

RANKINGS OF COMPANIES WITHIN INDUSTRIES

What are the leading companies in an industry? There are several sources that specifically address this, notably, Forbes rankings, Fortune 500, and Gale's *Business Rankings Annual.* Additionally, trade journals cover various industries—searching the databases will locate articles with rankings of companies within industry-specific journals.

Business Rankings Annual. Farmington Hills, MI: The Gale Group, 1989–
> (print) (http://www.gale.cengage.com/pdf/facts/BRAonGDL.pdf).
> Lists industries in alphabetical order—data compiled from trade journals for these specific industries. The *Business Rankings Annual* has general industries listed (banking) and specific as well (e.g., tableware, ice cream, and milk). Each entry provides the ranking title, lists the criteria (ranked by sales, revenue, and so on), and generally lists the top 10. To allow further research, *Business Rankings Annual* provides a citation for the source of the

data and a bibliography of resources. The online equivalent allows key word searches and compiling lists through exporting to Microsoft Word or Excel. Entries include hot-linked websites and email addresses.

Forbes—Forbes Lists (http://www.forbes.com/lists).
  Rankings feature the Forbes Global 2000, the ranking of the world's biggest companies, rated by composites of sales, profits, assets, and market value. Provides list of companies by category (industry) (http://www.forbes.com/lists/results.jhtml?bktDisplayField=stringfield3&bktDisplayField Length=3&passListId=18&passYear=2004&passListType=Company& searchParameter1=unset&searchParameter2=unset&resultsStart=1& resultsHowMany=100&resultsSortProperties=%2Bstringfield3%2C %2Bnumberfield1&resultsSortCategoryName=category&passKeyword =&category1=category&category2=category&fromColumnClick=true).

Fortune 500 (http://www.fortune.com). (http://money.cnn.com/magazines/fortune/fortune500/2010/industries).
  Features its annual Fortune 500, a benchmark in evaluating how companies perform within industries. The Fortune 500 allows researchers to determine the most successful companies within specific industries.

LOCATING INDUSTRY RATIOS

The performance of a company within a specific industry category is a staple of company/industry research. The industry ratios are used as a basis of determining a company's financial performance as related to its industry's financial average. Dun & Bradstreet provides the following definition: "key business ratios the relationship between financial values in a company's balance sheet and income statement" (https://www.dnb.com/ebir/help/key_biz_ratios.htm).

There are three major resources to be examined: the *Almanac of Business and Industrial Financial Ratios*, *Industry Norms and Key Business Ratios*, and *RMA Annual Statement Studies*.

Industry ratio books are designed for business professionals, faculty, and students. Academic libraries supporting a business school and larger public libraries should consider purchasing all three of the sources listed in this section.

Almanac of Business and Industrial Financial Ratios, by Leo Troy. Chicago: Prentice Hall. Annual.
  Provides 50 performance indicators for approximately 200 industries. Information derived from latest available IRS data on U.S. and international companies. Includes NAICS data for North America, Canada, and Mexico. An explanation of each component of the analysis for industries is explained in the preface. The table of contents lists industry categories based on NAICS. The contents follow the order of industries as arranged by the NAICS classification. Each entry provides total number of

enterprises (by money amounts and size of assets in thousands of dollars); revenues (in thousands), operation cost/operating income, selected average balance sheet, selected financial ratios (current, quick, net sales to working capital, coverage, total asset turnover, inventory turnover, receivable turnover, total liabilities to net worth, current assets to working capital, and so on), and selected financial factors (net ratio, return in total assets, and so on). Each entry contains 13 benchmarks, including receipts to cash flow, debt to total assets, and return on equity, and before and after taxes. The print edition is sent with a CD enabling users to input company data to see how it compares with the industry.

Industry Norms and Key Business Ratios. Center Valley, PA: Dun & Bradstreet. Annual. Available as online database Key Business Ratios (http://kbr.dnb.com/login/KBRHome.asp).

There are several editions of this source. Academic libraries supporting a program in business administration may want to consider the Desk Top Edition which is often suitable for use by students in completing assignments on how to find business ratios. The Desk Top Edition covers over 800 different lines of business arranged by SIC code numbers. General data are supplied via the Desk Top Edition. Dun & Bradstreet also publishes an expanded set (for corporation use) of books on industry norms and key business ratios covering the following segments: 1. Agriculture, Mining Construction/Transportation/Communication/Utilities. 2. Manufacturing; 3. Wholesaling; 4. Retailing; and 5. Finance/Real Estate Services. The expanded edition is available in a Three Year Edition (print and online) and One Year Edition (print and online). In the Desk Top Edition, the formulas for the ratios are provided and explained, and a preface on how to analyze the data is included. The source is arranged by SIC codes in numerical order (the Appendix lists the SIC codes used). For each entry, financials are provided, followed by the ratios (solvency, efficiency, and profitability) with upper quartile (UQ), median (Med), and lower quartile (LQ). Dun & Bradstreet provides online editions of the various formats of the industry norms and key business ratios.

RMA Annual Statement Studies. Philadelphia: Risk Management Association, Annual.

Organized using the NAICS system, *RMA Annual Statement Studies* contains data for over 750 industries—arranged within broad industry categories (e.g., Agriculture, Forestry, and Fishing and Hunting) and sub-categories, among which are Soybean Farming, Wheat Farming, and Corn Farming. The preface explains each ratio formula and how it is compiled and a guide on how to interpret the data. Data presented for each category include Assets, Liabilities, Income Data, Ratios (Current, Quick, Sales/Receivables, Cost of Sales/Inventory, and Cost of Sales Payables), and Sales Working Capital. The Risk Management Association also contains a website (http://www.statementstudies.org) that provides links to training programs on how to use and interpret the Statement Studies and provides access to information from the Annual Statement Studies and also regional breakouts of the data.

3

Information about Companies

INTRODUCTION

Locating company information is one of the most prevalent research tasks of individuals, ranging from students of business administration to potential buyers of stocks to those investigating a specific product or service of a company to those comparing companies within specific industries. The Internet has made this research more efficient; many databases were formerly in print only, and the company annual reports previously in paper or microform and government 10K reports are now readily accessible in digital format. This chapter is limited to locating data about companies; a discussion of obtaining and using resources on locating stock and bond prices is located in chapters on investing.

TYPES OF COMPANIES

Public Companies

Public companies are those that have shareholders in the company with stocks sold to the public. Disclosure laws by the federal government require that that public companies file annual and other required reports to the U.S. Securities and Exchange Commission (SEC) and to shareholders in the company. Therefore, public company information is readily available, and researchers have various options to locate annual and other reports, including through the SEC website (the 10K annual reports that are more detailed than the annual reports to shareholders) and via the companies' own websites (reports to shareholders and investors will contain the annual report plus SEC filings).

Private Companies

Privately held or closely held companies are those that do not sell shares of stock to the general public. These companies do not have the disclosure requirements that public companies have. Therefore, this information is not as readily available, although some provide financial data to publishers of directories (online and print), and some private companies' websites provide information. See the discussion of publishers and periodical databases for further coverage

Subsidiaries or Subsidiary Companies

Subsidiary companies are owned by a parent company that controls the operations. Information about subsidiary companies are provided on the parent companies' websites and/or publishers, such as Hoover's. See the discussion of company directories and periodical databases for further coverage.

SOURCES OF PUBLIC COMPANY ANNUAL REPORTS

Annual Reports to Shareholders

Annual reports provide information to shareholders in a company and/or anyone interested in the company. The public company annual report in print and online is generally in color and has visuals and illustrations of the company's products (if applicable) and photographs of the chief executive officers (CEOs) and key officers. The report to shareholders contains a letter from the CEO, who reports on developments in the company, including any new product/services launches; financial data; results of continuing operations; projections for the future; and market segmentation information.

Public Company Websites

Although generally public companies still offer the traditional print annual reports that may be requested directly by researchers via snail mail, the Internet has added a new dimension to distributing data to researchers and shareholders. Public companies may be located via a search on Google, Yahoo!, or other search engines. In addition, the URLs of public companies are generally included in company directories. On the home page generally, the annual reports are listed under "information for investors." If there is no link, select "site map" on the home page to locate the specific link to annual reports and SEC filings. In addition to the annual report information, researchers can find out about new product and service lines and news about the company. Subsidiary companies reports may be found as a separate URL or under the parent company's website.

It should be noted that many private companies have websites but generally do not contain the full degree of data that public companies furnish to investors.

Annual and Other Reports Filed with the SEC

A public company is required by law to file forms with the SEC. Researchers who limit their study of a company to its 10K annual report will find that it is a black-and-white document in plain text without the visuals of the company's annual report to shareholders and are more detailed. If a shareholder requests a 10K report from the company, it is required by law to mail this to the shareholder.

The contents as set out by the SEC for the 10K must contain a description of, among others, business, risk factors, and properties; legal proceedings; financial statements; management's discussion and analysis of financial conditions and results of operations; directors, executive officers, and corporate governance; executive compensation; principal accounting fees and services; and quantitative and qualitative disclosures about market risk.

U.S. Securities and Exchange Commission (SEC) (http://www.sec.gov).
    A public company is required by law to file forms with the SEC. Researchers who limit their study of a company to its 10K report will find that it is a black-and-white document in plain text without the visuals of the company's annual report to shareholders and are more detailed.

    The 10K reports are available directly from the U.S. government's SEC/ Edgar site. However, the SEC lists other types of reports that may be of interest to researchers of a company.

Types of Forms filed with the SEC

Submission Type	Description
1-E, 1-E/A	Notification under Regulation E by small business investment companies and business development companies.
1-E AD, 1-E AD/A	Sales material filed pursuant to Rule 607 under Regulation E.
2-E, 2-E/A	Report of sales of securities pursuant to Rule 609 under Regulation E.
10-12B, 10-12B/A	Initial general form for registration of a class of securities pursuant to section 12(b)
10-12G, 10-12G/A	Initial general form for registration of a class of securities pursuant to section 12(g)
10-D, 10-D/A	Periodic distribution reports by Asset-Backed issuers pursuant to Rule 13a-17 or 15d-17
10-K, 10-K/A	Annual report pursuant to section 13 and 15(d)
10KSB, 10KSB/A	Optional form for annual and transition reports of small business issuers under section 13 or 15(d) Will no longer be accepted as of March 16, 2009
10-KT, 10-KT/A	Transition report pursuant to Rule 13a-10 or 15d-10
10-Q, 10-Q/A	Quarterly report pursuant to sections 13 or 15(d)
10-QT, 10-QT/A	Transition report pursuant to Rule 13a-10 or 15d-10
11-K, 11-K/A	Annual report of employee stock purchase, savings and similar plans
11-KT, 11-KT/A	Transition report pursuant to rule 13a-10 or 15d10
13F-HR, 13F-HR/A	Initial Quarterly Form 13F Holdings report filed by institutional managers
13F-NT, 13F-NT/A	Initial Quarterly Form 13F Notice Report filed by institutional managers
144, 144/A	Filing for proposed sale of securities under Rule 144
15-12B, 15-12B/A	Notice of termination of registration of a class of securities under Section 12(b)
15-12G, 15-12G/A	Notice of termination of registration of a class of securities under Section 12(g)
15-15D, 15-15D/A	Notice of suspension of duty to file reports

Source: **From SEC/Edgar website.**

Company Directories and Data Sources

There are publishers that have provided company data, whether in providing extensive reports to names and addresses and "quick" facts only. With these publishers now generally providing both print and nonprint sources, obtaining this information is easily accessible and searchable by researchers.

Dun & Bradstreet (http://www.dnb.com/us).

>Dun & Bradstreet offers a wide array of services related to company information, and its database product Dun & Bradstreet's *Million Dollar Database* (http://www.dnbmdd.com/mddi) enables searching by company and industry. Its advanced search capability allows users to limit by public/private, industry, executives, North American Industry Classification System (NAICS) or Standard Industrial Classification (SIC) codes, location, and size (sales, employment). Entries for companies include D-U-N-S (Dun's Universal Numbering System) number, name, address, telephone number, plant/facility size, Web address, ticker symbol, number of employees, executives, executive biographies, NAICS, SIC, line of business, and products. It should be noted that the D-U-N-S number is assigned to a business establishment by Dun & Bradstreet to be used as a numeric identifier for business location.

Hoover's (http://www.hoovers.com).

>Hoover's offers both print and nonprint materials, although many libraries now have "gone digital" and opted to subscribe to Hoover's online edition only. Hoover's focuses on both company and industry information and contains not only public company but also selected private company data. Biographical entries are provided as well for officers. Those searching Hoover's can browse by industries to browse companies or conduct company searches. A search for General Electric, for example, yields the name and address, telephone number, website, company overview, ranking of this company by Fortune 500, key people, leading competitors, financial data, list of CEO and officers with some biographical data, primary SIC and NAICS codes, news releases, and stock quotes. To determine the type of company, users can conduct an advance search to limit to type of company (private, public, subsidiary) and specify specific search criteria: auditors, company size, and company criteria, among other categories.

The following are print titles for Hoover's:

Hoover's Handbook of American Business. Austin, TX: Hoover's. Annual.
>Profiles 750 U.S. companies.

Hoover's Handbook of World Business. Austin, TX: Hoover's. Annual.
>Profiles 300 companies outside the United States.

Hoover's Handbook of Private Companies. Austin, TX: Hoover's. Annual.
>Covers 900 of the largest private U.S. business enterprises.

Hoover's Handbook of Emerging Companies. Austin, TX: Hoover's. Annual.
>Profiles 600 U.S. growth companies.

LexisNexis Academic Universe (http://www.lexisnexis.com).

>LexisNexis Academic Universe contains a company research section. On the first screen, select the "Companies" tab, and there are various files to search: SEC filings, Lexis Nexis Company Dossiers, Dossier Compare Companies, and Dossier Create a Company list. Company profiles provide full text regarding companies from various online publications, among which are Disclosure, Nelson's Public Company profiles, and

Standard & Poor's, among other sources, Lexis Nexis Dossier provides in-depth data on both private and public companies.

Mergent Online (formerly Moody's) (http://www.mergent.com).
This database allows searching of both public and private companies. Results of searches yield name, address, stock ticker, website, number of employees, number of shareholders, summary of business, key financials, company news, competitors, and so on. It also offers digital back files of the print Mergent Manuals, allowing for company research decades back. The digital back files contain *Industrial Manual* since 1920, *OTC Industrial* Manual since 1970, *OTC Unlisted Manual* since 1985, *Bank and Finance Manual* since 1928, *Public Utility Manual* since 1914, *Transportation Manual* since 1909, and *International Manual* since 1981. Additionally, Mergent offers a Global Private Company Database featuring over 20 million private companies with key company information.

Standard & Poor's (a McGraw-Hill Company) (http://www.standardand poors.com/home/en/us).
Standard and Poor's Register has long been a staple for Company research. Standard & Poor's now features the database *NetAdvantage* (http://www.netadvantage.standardandpoors.com/NASApp/NetAdvantage/index.do), which brings together its diverse range of products formerly found only in print formats. Researchers of company data can go to the main page and select the "Company" tab. Once on the Company page, users can search registers of both private and public companies and opt for these specific searches or just opt to do a key word search. A search of General Electric in the company register yields the name, address, sales, stock data, ticker symbol primary SIC and NAICS codes, and officers and directors. Researchers can also scroll to Company Profile to find a "snapshot" of the business summary and company fact sheet.

Thomson Reuters Web Disclosure (http://thomsonreuters.com).
Thomson Reuters Web Disclosure provides coverage of approximately 15,000 public companies and reports derived from SEC files. It features coverage of annual and quarterly report data, including balance sheets, income statements, ratios, full text of management discussion, and president's letter to stockholders.

Periodical Indexes and Full-Text Databases

A thorough search on a company should include periodical articles. For instance, through these articles, researchers can find out the following: what has General Motors planned since it published its last annual report, how have sales been for the company, and who are the corporate officers of the company? Additionally, those researching privately held companies may find articles about these companies and provide much needed data not found in directories. Journals and newspapers, including

Harvard Business Review, Forbes, Fortune, Barron's, and *BusinessWeek,* all offer profiles of companies, whether it be a biography of a leading CEO, a discussion of a new product or service, or an analysis of a company's performance. Online databases allow searching to locate articles about companies and focus on specific issues related to these companies.

Researchers of periodical articles for company information can search *ABI/INFORM, Business Source Premier, Wilson Business Periodicals Index, Wilson Business Abstracts,* and *Wilson Business Full Text, ScienceDirect,* and *JSTOR.* For a complete description of these databases, see Chapter 2.

Periodicals and Newspapers

In addition to the following, researchers should consult specific industry trade journals to locate articles on the companies in those industries.

Barron's (http://online.barrons.com/home-page)
Bloomberg Businessweek (http://www.businessweek.com)
Financial Times (http://www.ft.com/home/uk)
Forbes (http://www.forbes.com)
Fortune (http://money.cnn.com/magazines/fortune)
Harvard Business Review (http://hbr.org)
Wall Street Journal (http://online.wsj.com/home-page)

Books about Company Histories

Those who want to delve into company information and go back to the origins and what happened during the past decades should examine the databases *WorldCat* and *Books in Print* to check the literature on the companies. Especially of interest are memoirs of company officers and founders; for instance, books by Martha Stewart, Donald Trump, Bill Gates, and Lee Iacocca provide unique insights and data that are especially valuable.

International Directory of Company Histories (http://www.gale.cengage.com/
  pdf/facts/CompanyHist.pdf).
  Thomson Gale features a set of volumes in both print and digital formats
  that presents histories of the company. The multivolume print set contains cumulative indexes with each volume so that researchers can
  readily obtain the entry or entries for the company. It is important to note
  that "key" companies often receive updated entries in this directory. Each
  entry contains the company logo, address, phone number, website, ticker
  symbol, sales to date, and history of the company.

  The online database *International Directory of Company Histories* enables key
  word searching and accesses all the directory entries in full text that relate
  to a particular company.

Other sources of historical information can be found by searching databases (listed above) as well as back issues of newspapers, notably the *New York Times* and the *Wall Street Journal*.

Also check the company websites, some of which do provide a history and background of a company.

Historical Company Annual Reports

Columbia University Historical Corporate Annual Reports Collection Digitized Annual Reports from the Watson Library's Collection (http://www.columbia.edu/cu/lweb/indiv/business/CorpReports.html).
Focusing on companies in and around New York City, this searchable database provides digitized historical annual reports.

4

Personal Finance and Investing— Introductory Sources and Guides

Investing for consumers often means putting away a "nest egg" for retirement, saving money for their children's college education, setting aside a fund for retirement, or saving for a home. What consumers invest in takes many forms: stocks, bonds, mutual funds, certificates of deposit, commodities, real estate, and other investments that may include buying art and antiques and collecting stamps and coins.

This chapter is an overview of investing and describes resources that feature practical advice on choosing and planning investments. In addition, resources are described that focus on personal financial planning.

ENCYCLOPEDIAS AND DICTIONARIES

Bach, David. *The Finish Rich Dictionary: 1000 Financial Words You Need to Know*. New York: Oxford University Press, 2009.

A practical dictionary for investors and for business students. Defines terms (includes pronunciation key) including lump sum, escrow, bull market, Sallie Mae, capital gain, and wholesale. In addition to the definition, the author provides chapters of specific help to investors/consumers: "How to Determine if You Have a Credit Card Problem," "Understanding Your Credit Score," and "How to Buy a Home." Also features a bibliography, a listing of common financial equations, and an interest rate calculator table.

Bonham, Howard Bryan. *The Complete Investment and Financial Dictionary*. Hillbrook, MA: Adams Media Corporation, 2002.

Defines terms of finance, investment, estate planning, economics, law, and accounting. Includes cross-references. In addition, lists information sources (trade associations; books, periodicals, and subscription services; and Internet sites).

Downes, John, and Jordan Elliot Goodman. *Dictionary of Finance and Investment Terms*. 8th ed. Hauppauge, NY: Barron's Educational Series, 2010.
Contains definitions of approximately 5,000 terms related to finance and investment and includes terms related to various types of investments from stocks to collectibles. Features cross-references and abbreviations and acronyms.

GUIDES

General Investment Guides

CNN Money.com Money 101 (http://money.cnn.com/magazines/money mag/money101).
Series of lessons for investors; topics include setting priorities, making a budget, basics of banking and saving, basics of investing, investing in stocks, investing in bonds, investing in mutual funds, buying a home, and planning for retirement, and taxes.

Downes, John, and Jordan Goodman. *Barron's Finance and Investment Handbook*. 8th ed. Hauppauge, NY: Barron's Educational Series, 2010.
Practical guide to personal investment opportunities features: a dictionary of 5,000 key terms; directory of brokerage firms, mutual funds, investment newsletters and magazines, financial institutions, and regulators; and directory of 600 corporations. Features historical financial data. Contains descriptions and evaluations of various types of investments, including securities, real estate, and collectibles. Contains extensive annotated bibliography for further research.

Fisher, Ken, with Lara Hoffmans. *How to Smell a Rat: The Five Signs of Financial Fraud*. Hoboken, NJ: Wiley, 2009.
Practical guide that alerts investors about the warning signs of fraud. Uses example of fraud from real life, including the Bernie Madoff case. Author advice to readers includes basic principles, such as "too good to be true usually is" and "due diligence is your job, no one else's." Contains a biography for further research.

Fragasso, Phil, and Craig L. Israelsen. *Your Nest Egg Game Plan: How to Get Your Finances Back on Track and Create a Lifetime Income Stream*. Franklin Lakes, NJ: Career Press, 2009.
Focuses on financial planning for retirement. Examines cycles of life and money, strategies for building a nest egg, planning for retirement, keeping pace with the cost of living, and lifestyle options for retirement and features case studies.

Hinden, Stan. *How To Retire Happy: The 12 Most Important Decisions You Must Make before You Retire*. 3rd ed. New York: McGraw-Hill, 2010.
Offers practical advice on planning for retirement. Discusses social security concerns, individual retirement accounts, investing after retirement,

health insurance, determining where to live after retirement, health insurance, and wills and estates.

Investopedia (http://www.investopedia.com).
Guide to personal finance and investing options. Features a glossary of terms related to finance and investing, with definitions, cross-references, and a list of related links.

The Investor's Clearinghouse (Alliance for Investor Education) (http://www.investoreducation.org).
Features a wide variety of investment advice and contains news releases; advice and resources about bonds, stocks, and mutual funds; avoiding scams; investing basics; and future and financing planning.

Kiplinger.com (http://www.kiplinger.com).
Offers guides to investing, taxes, insurance, retirement planning, family finance, and credit and money management. Also features podcasts that are included: "Where to Invest in 2011" and "12 Secrets to Boost Your 401(k)."

Lim, Paul J. *Investing Demystified*. New York: McGraw-Hill, 2005.
Guide to investing in various assets. Discusses how to invest, select and organize assets, and analyze specific investments, among which are stocks, bonds, mutual funds, real estate, and precious metals. Examines research resources and features a glossary of terms.

Malkiel, Burton G., and Charles D. Ellis. *The Elements of Investing*. Hoboken, NJ: Wiley, 2010.
Introductory guide to the basics of investing. Offers advice on personal finance and specific advice, including building up savings, taxation considerations, and advice on the allocation of assets.

Orman, Suze. *The Road to Wealth: A Comprehensive Guide to Your Money: Everything You Need to Know in Good and Bad Times*. New York: Riverhead Books, 2008.
Suze Orman, who is a major personal finance expert and adviser, has written numerous financial planning guides and has appeared on television offering advice. This guide offers advice on money management and covers topics of managing debt, insurance, paying for college, annuities, retirement planning, investing in stocks, home ownership, and investing in bonds. For additional, up-to-date information from Orman, her website, http://www.suzeorman.com, is recommended for additional guidance on various aspects of personal finance, including a will and trust tool kit, an identity theft kit, announcements of Orman's appearances on television and radio, and a list of books by Orman for sale.

Tyson, Eric. *Investing for Dummies*. 5th ed. Hoboken, NJ: Wiley, 2008.
Offers practical advice on investments in stocks, bonds, mutual funds, collectibles, and real estate plus guidance in starting a small business. Features selecting the best books, periodicals, and Internet resources.

U.S. Securities and Exchange Commission, Office of Investor Education and
   Advocacy (http://www.sec.gov/investor.shtml).
   Provides a guide for investors regarding how to check out brokers and
   advisers, tips and complaints, how to avoid scams, and guides to specific
   types of investments (e.g., hedge funds, insurance, stocks, and bonds)
   and recent rule making and topics of interest to investors. Among the
   available online publications are "For Seniors: Protect Yourselves against
   Investment Fraud" and "Questions You Should Ask about Your Investments." Publishes a printed guide for beginning investors: *Saving and
   Investing: A Roadmap to Your Financial Security through Saving and Investing*
   and *A Guide for Seniors: Protect Yourself against Investment Fraud*.

Yahoo! Finance—Personal Finance (http://finance.yahoo.com/personal
   -finance).
   Guide to personal financial management features news releases, advice on
   retirement planning, personal finances, saving for college, and links to
   Yahoo! guides on specific types of investments (e.g., stocks and mutual
   funds).

GUIDES TO SPECIFIC INVESTMENTS NOT COVERED
IN OTHER, RELATED CHAPTERS

The following are selected guides to investments, including stamps,
coins, antiques, and collectibles. It should be noted that there are specific
guides on the market for other investments, among which are wines,
toys, baseball cards, and celebrity autographs, to name only a few.
Researchers should consult the *Encyclopedia of Associations* for specific
organizations or clubs related to these investments for further research.

The Antiques Roadshow Online (http://www.pbs.org/wgbh/roadshow).
   Features video archives of appraisals, a schedule of future shows on PBS,
   and online appraisals with features on specific types of antiques and
   collectibles.

Hudgeons, Thomas, Jr. *The Official Blackbook Price Guide to United States Postage
   Stamps*. New York: House of Collectibles. Annual.
   Illustrated guides provides review of market with current trends in investing; prices for first-day cover, mint sheets, and plate blocks; and guide to
   buying and selling at auctions.

Kloetzel, James E. *Scott Specialized Catalogue of United States Stamps and Covers*.
   New York: Scott Publishing Co. Annual.
   Coverage includes values of first-day covers, airmail, proofs, U.S. possessions stamps, plate blocks, computer-vended postage, Confederate States
   stamps, revenue stamps, and telegraph stamps. Definitive stamp-
   collecting source for investors and collectors. Scott Publishing Co. also
   features catalogs for stamps from overseas.

Kovel, Terry. *Kovels' Antique and Collectibles Price Guide: America's Most Authoritative Antiques Annual*. New York: Black Dog and Leventhal Publishers. Annual.

Lists prices actually obtained over the past year for a wide variety of collectibles and antiques. Features 2,500 color photographs and over 700 categories, including sports memorabilia, pottery and porcelain, jewelry, furniture, and glassware. Features a website (http://www.kovels.com) that, in addition to price guides, includes a directory of appraisal services, auctions, museums and archives, and clubs and publications.

Moran, Mark F. *Warman's Antiques and Collectibles Price Guide* Iola, WI: Krause Publications. Annual.

For those investing in antiques and collectibles, the author provides a description of the state of the market for collecting and a list of prices (compiled from information from auction houses and dealers) for a wide variety of antiques and collectibles, including comic books, Royal Doulton figurines, baseball cards, toys, and furniture. Items are illustrated.

U.S. Postal Service. *The Postal Service Guide to U.S. Stamps*. New York: Harper-Collins. Annual.

Guide for collectors and investors, an identification guide to U.S. stamps, including commemorative stamps, airmail stamps, duck stamps, and stamped envelopes.

Yeoman, R. S. *A Guide Book of United States Coins: The Official Red Book*. Edited by Kenneth Bressett. Atlanta: Whitman Publishing. Annual.

For the intermediate to advanced collectors, coin dealers, auctioneers, and investors, provides descriptions and illustrations of U.S. coins from colonial times to the present. Covers early, rare proof coins, updated pricing records, auction records, and silver, gold, and platinum bullion coins. Whitman Publishing's website (http://www.whitmanbooks.com), in addition to listing its publications for sale, features coins and stamps for sale to collectors.

INVESTOR ADVISORY AND PROTECTION AGENCIES

The following agencies safeguard and protect investments.

AARP (American Association of Retired Persons) (http://www.aarp.org).

Nonprofit, nonpartisan membership organization that helps people 50 and over improve the quality of their lives. Features a "Money" section, which offers advice on how to avoid financial scams and on investing and retirement planning, Social Security, estate planning, taxes, and insurance. The "Money Tools" section covers investing, budgeting/saving, retirement planning, and so on. AARP publishes the journals *AARP Bulletin* and *AARP: The Magazine*.

Financial Industry Regulatory Authority (FINRA) (http://www.finra.org).
    FINRA is an advocate for investors and enforces high ethical standards,
    governing activities of approximately 4,700 brokerage firms. Offers
    advice to investors on how to protect their money and avoid scams and
    advises on choosing investments and retirement plans. Features a Retire-
    ment Made Simpler Campaign, conducted jointly with AARP and the
    Retirement Security Project, providing information and rsources related
    to retirement plans. Also features Generation Money, an educational pro-
    gram for financial education for teens.

U.S. Securities and Exchange Commission (http://www.sec.gov)

See Chapter 5 for description.

DIRECTORY

Standard & Poor's Security Dealers of North America. Charlottesville, VA: Stan-
    dard & Poor's. Issued in spring and fall.
    Entries are arranged in a geographical-alphabetical sequence; also
    included are three index sections: Firm Name Changes Section, Discon-
    tinued Listings Section, and Location of Investment Firms Section. Each
    entry contains name, address, telephone, officers, number of employees,
    and class of securities in which the firm specializes (when available).
    Nature of the firm is categorized by terms: brokers, participating distrib-
    utors, underwriters, originators, and stockbrokers.

PERIODICAL INDEXES AND FULL-TEXT DATABASES

Recommended databases are *ABI/INFORM, Business Source Premier*
(EBSCOhost), and *Wilsonline Business Periodicals Index* and general
databases, including *Academic Search Premier* (EBSCO Host) and *Pro-
Quest Newspapers*. See Chapter 2 for complete description of major
databases.

PERIODICALS

AARP: The Magazine (http://www.aarp.org/magazine)
Barron's (http://online.wsj.com/home-page)
Bloomberg Businessweek (http://www.businessweek.com)
Forbes (http://www.forbes.com/forbes)
Fortune (http://money.cnn.com/magazines/fortune)
Investment News (http://www.investmentnews.com)
Journal of Consumer Affairs (http://www.wiley.com/bw/journal.asp?ref
    =0022-0078)

Journal of Financial Planning (http://www.fpanet.org/journal)
Kiplinger's Personal Finance (http://www.kiplinger.com)
Money Magazine (http://money.cnn.com/magazines/moneymag)
Pensions and Investments (http://www.pionline.com)
Smart Money (http:///www.smartmoney.com)
Wall Street Journal (http://online.wsj.com/home-page)

5

The Stock Market

A stock can be defined as "an ownership share or ownership shares in a company". (Scott, *Wall Street Words*). Stocks are traded through national and regional exchanges, most notably including the New York Stock Exchange and NASDAQ. Common stocks are those where investors receive dividends and have voting rights, and preferred stocks are those where investors have priority over common stockholders in payment of dividends and have no voting rights.

The roots of the current stock exchanges were in Europe in the twelfth century. In France in the twelfth century, the "courratiers de change" met to manage agricultural debts on behalf of the banks and also traded in debts. Another early forerunner to current exchange was in fourteenth-century Italy.

In the United States on May 17, 1792, the New York Stock Exchange (its earliest name was the New York Stock and Exchange Board) was founded via the signing of an agreement under a buttonwood tree at 68 Wall Street. The original Buttonwood Tree Agreement is found in the archives of the New York Stock Exchange. The name of the exchange became the New York Stock Exchange in 1863.

Other major exchanges subsequently were formed both nationally and regional. Some of the world's major stock exchanges include NASDAQ (http://www.nasdaq.com), the New York Stock Exchange (http://www.nyse.com), the London Stock Exchange (http://www.londonstockexchange.com/home/homepage.htm), the Tokyo Stock Exchange (http://www.tse.or.jp/english), the Chicago Stock Exchange (http://www.chx.com), and the Hong Kong Exchange. For a list of major stock exchanges by country, see Appendix IV.

DIRECTORY

Stock and Commodity Exchange Directories (Rutgers University Library)
(http://libguides.rutgers.edu/stocks).
 Locate links to stock exchanges in the United States, Canada, Europe, Asia
 and Australasia, Latin America and the Caribbean, the Middle East, and
 Canada.

ENCYCLOPEDIAS AND DICTIONARIES

The following provide key definitions of terminology. It should be
noted that the stock exchanges have glossaries of terms for investors.

Downes, John. *Dictionary of Finance and Investment Terms*. 8th ed. Hauppauge,
 NY: Barron's Educational Series, Inc., 2010.
 Defines terms on finance and investing, including those related to stocks.

International Encyclopedia of the Stock Market. Edited by Michael Sheimo.
 Chicago: Fitzroy Dearborn Publishers, 1999. 2 volumes.
 Provides definitions of approximately 2,000 terms related to the regional,
 national, and overseas stock markets. Defines terms, events, organizations, and countries (stock exchange entries are listed within their location;
 e.g., the London Stock Exchange is listed under the entry for the United
 Kingdom). Cross-references are included.

Pessin, Allan H., and Joseph A. Ross. *The Complete Words of Wall Street: The
 Professional's Guide to Investment Literacy*. Homewood, IL: Business One
 Irwin, 1991.
 Definitions of terms on investing, including stock-related terms: "New
 York Stock Exchange (NYSE)," "bull market," "blue chip," and "bear
 market." Cross-referenced.

Peterson, Nora. *Wall Street Lingo: Thousands of Investment Terms Explained Simply*.
 Ocala, FL: Atlantic Publishing Co., 2007.
 A dictionary containing definitions of terms, organizations (including
 stock exchanges)—definitions are arranged within specific categories,
 such as Market Mechanics (the Exchanges, Exchange Operations, and
 Playing Fair: Rules and Regulations), Who's Who (including investors
 and regulatory authorities), Market Forces (economics for investors),
 and Asset Classes (stocks, bonds, options, futures, and initial public offerings). Also features a guide to abbreviations, a bibliography, and a list of
 Internet resources.

Scott, David L. *Wall Street Words: The Essential A to Z Guide for Today's Investor*.
 Boston: Houghton Mifflin, 1997.
 Definitions related to stocks and other investments—including terminology,
 stock exchanges, and so on. Includes a "Technical Analysis Chart Patterns"
 section with samples of statistical charts used for investment data.

Shook, R. J., and Robert L. Shook. *The Wall Street Dictionary.* New York: New
York Institute of Finance, 1990.
Contains definitions, including those related to stock markets and investing.

HOW TO FIND STOCK PRICES, DOW JONES INDUSTRIAL AVERAGE, STANDARD & POOR'S 500, AND OTHER DATA

A major concern of investors and those interested in the health of the
stock market is locating stock prices and other statistics about the markets. The Internet has made it possible to obtain real-time stock quotes
rather than delayed reports of stocks. There are a multitude of resources
on locating stock exchange averages and quotes. Additionally, there are
selected specific data related to the stock markets.

Included among this list are sources such as *Value Line Investment
Survey* and *Standard & Poor's Stock Reports,* which also provide recom-
mendations to investors as to whether to buy, sell, or hold the stock.
Among these are the following:

Dow Jones Industrial Average (DJIA)—The oldest price measure in con-
tinuous use, founded on May 26, 1896, by Charles H. Dow. It is an index
of movement of price movements in the market for industrial-type
stock. The majority of the stocks included in the DJIA are listed on the
NYSE—companies represented are "blue chip."

Dow Jones Transportation Average—Measures price movements in the
transportation sector of the U.S. economy.

Dow Jones Utility Average—Measures price movements in the utility sector
of the U.S. economy.

Dow Jones Composite Average—Measures price changes in the three major
economic sectors in the United States: industrial, transportation, and utility.

Standard & Poor's 500 Index (S&P 500)—Compiled by S&P, measures
price trend movements based on the capitalization-weighted index of
500 stocks.

SOURCES OF STOCK QUOTES AND RELATED DATA

Barron's (http://online.barrons.com/home-page) (published by Dow Jones &
Company).
Features stock quotes, "picks and pans" of various stocks, the "Stock-
Grader" analysis of stock performance, Barron's Market Data Center
(with real-time quotes), the "Barron's 400 Index," and news for investors.
Print and online formats. Also available through ProQuest.

Big Charts.com, a service of MarketWatch (http://bigcharts.marketwatch.com).
Provides current stock market data, including major market indexes and
financial news. Search by ticker symbol or key word of a company to

obtain a basic chart of its market data, including current price. Site contains a ticker symbol look-up feature. Select links above the chart to obtain additional information about the company—current news, industry information, market advisers' reports on the company, analyst estimates, annual report, technical analysis, Securities and Exchange Commission filings, message board (requires registration), company description (including valuation ratios, price-earnings ratios, per share data, officers and executives, and profitability)—and add to portfolio and set up the alerts feature (requires registration) and Hulbert analysis (analysis by investment advisers—requires registration). The Advanced Chart allows searching by parameters: provides a time frame and allows users to choose a chart style. The Interactive Chart allows more options in creating format for data presentation, including price display, upper indicators, and trend lines.

Bloomberg.com (http://www.bloomberg.com).
   In addition to stock data, and key indicators, Bloomberg provides: news reports, editorial opinion, and guide to investing, profiles of companies and CEOs, economic news, etc.

Bloomberg Professional: Equities (http://www.bloomberg.com/professional/equities/)
   A financial services system that provides data in real time and provides users the ability to create custom charts for single or multiple securities and view spreads or ratios. Provides data on historical and intraday price records for common stocks and options, and SEC filings as well as company data, including dividend, earnings, and shareholder, and examine company data on cash flow, income statements, and balance sheets.

CNNMoney.com (http://money.cnn.com).
   Provides latest news alerts regarding the stock market and business news in general. Search by ticker symbol to locate real-time stock quotes, today's change (negative or positive), year-to-date performance, 52-week price range, five-day price change chart, and latest headlines involving the specific company.

CRSP—Center for Research in Security Prices, U.S. Stock Database (http://www.crsp.com).
   Contains end-of-day and month-end prices on all listed NYSE (data series begin December 31, 1925), AMEX (data series begin July 2, 1962), and NASDAQ common stocks (data series begin December 14, 1972) with basic market indices.

Capital IQ (COMPUSTAT) (http://www.compustat.com/myproducts.aspx).
   Source of financial and accounting data for over 25,000 public companies.

The Dow Jones Averages 1885–1995. Edited by Phyllis S. Pierce. Chicago: Irwin Professional Publishing, 1996.
   Describes the origins of the Dow Jones averages as developed by Charles Dow. Contains a chronology of the history, including listing companies used to compile the data (for each year used in this chronology). Each

year covered in the section on the Dow includes the day-to-day averages
with a monthly summary of the high and low compilations.

DAILY STOCK PRICE RECORDS (STANDARD & POOR'S)

The following sources (in print format) provide day-by-day stock quotes
with the volume, high, low, and closing prices. Published quarterly

Daily Stock Price Record. New York Stock Exchange. New York: Standard &
Poor's, 1962–.

Daily Stock Price Record. American Stock Exchange. New York: Standard &
Poor's, 1962.

Daily Stock Price Record. NASDAQ. New York: Standard & Poor's, 1993–.

Daily Stock Price Record. Over-the-Counter. New York: Standard & Poor's, 1973–1992.

Dow Jones Factiva (http://factiva.com).

For the researcher and investor, *Factiva* is a database containing access to
the following resources: current news from wire services; full-text access
to newspapers, among which are the *Wall Street Journal* and the *New York
Times*; key television and radio transcripts from ABC, CBS, NBC, Fox, and
CNN; and international newspapers. Also accessible through ProQuest.

Financial Times (London) (http://www.ft.com/home/us). Print and online
editions.

In addition to articles that analyze the market, features data on the S&P 500,
prices for American and British stocks, prices for other international
stocks (e.g., Australia, France, Spain, and Russia), stock market world
markets at a glance, stock market ratios, volatility indices, the FTSE Global
Equity Index Series, and the most active stocks and biggest movers for the
United States, London, Tokyo, and the Euro markets.

Investext (Thomson Research) (http://research.thomsonib.com).

Contains access to 35 investment report sources (of markets and companies worldwide).

Mergent Handbook of Common Stocks (http://www.mergent.com). Print and
digital formats.

To locate the online format, search for company and select stock reports
(fact sheets). Each report provides a recommendation (buy, sell, or hold)
and provides a business summary, analysis summary, chart of price performance, earnings momentum, analyst forecast, recent developments,
and quality rating.

Standard & Poor's Analysts' Handbook. New York: Standard & Poor's. Annual
and monthly editions.Available in print, Microsoft Access Database format, and on CD.

Provides data based on the S&P 500. Data are arranged within specific
industry categories, and statistics provided include per share data items,
price data, dividend data, and financials.

Standard & Poor's Dividend Record. New York: Standard & Poor's. Online and print.
   Features data on dividends paid for over 25,000 equity securities.

Standard & Poor's Stock Reports (http://www.netadvantage.standardand
   poors.com/NASApp/NetAdvantage/index.do).
   Available through its NetAdvantage database, the S&P Reports provide
   statistics and evaluations of stocks, with data on stock performance and
   projections. The S&P gives ratings by number of stars (five being the
   highest) and a recommendation of buy, hold, or sell. Each record contains
   the name and address, ticker symbol, summary of the company and
   background, industry sector, price of stock, chart of its price performance,
   financial data, industry and company performance analysis by the S&P
   and projections regarding stock and company performance, and press
   releases about the company. In "tear sheet" format, each reports provide
   highly detailed data and analysis by S&P analysts. The S&P provides
   "tours" and "guides" to the S&P Stock Guide for explanations on how
   data are compiled and interpreted. Also on the NetAdvantage home
   page, there is a "Stock of the Week" link focusing on a specific stock. On
   the "Stock of the Week" page, researchers can also see the "rising" and
   "falling" stars of stocks and new stocks. Also, the S&P Indexes are located
   on this page. A glossary of terms is included on NetAdvantage.

StockCharts.com (http://stockcharts.com/charts/index.html).
   Allows free access to chart creation tools; for more complex charts, a subscription is necessary. Lists: Most Active Stocks for the New York Stock
   Exchange, NASDAQ, and Toronto Stock Exchange. Search by key word
   or ticker symbol to locate charts. A chart is provided for each stock with
   researchers having access to update the chart by chart scale, prices, time
   periods, and chart overlays. Online instruction manuals are provided
   for the creation and updating of charts.

Stock Maven Research Center (http://www.stockmaven.com).
   Provides links to real-time stock quotes, 30 industrial stock components,
   custom quote tracking, earnings/dividends, and breaking news from
   Bloomberg.

Value Line Investment Survey (http://www.valueline.com).Print and online
   formats.
   A key source for investors in analyzing stocks and making investment
   decisions. This source is organized as follows: Ratings and Reports are
   comprised of 13 issues (each issue is updated every 13 weeks and features analysis of a specific company on a full-page report); each company
   covered provides current and historical data, three to five years of price
   and earnings projections, a description of the business, charts, financial
   data, analyst commentaries about the company's outlook, recent price,
   price-earnings ratio, and so on. Also in this section, Value Line announces
   the additions of new companies added since the last issue; a summary
   and index list companies analyzed and the page of the report; there is
   also an index of industries covered and tables categorizing stocks in various categories (highest-growth stocks, untimely stocks, highest-

dividend-yielding nonutility stocks, bargain-basement stock, best-performing stocks, worst-performing stocks, and so on); Selection & Opinion features analysis by experts in the field about current economic and market statistics and forecasts.

VALUE LINE SAMPLE PAGE

THE VALUE LINE Investment Survey®
www.valueline.com

Part 3
Ratings & Reports

ISSUE 1
Pages 100-242

File in the binder in order of issue number, removing previous issue bearing the same number.

February 27, 2009

ESPECIALLY NOTEWORTHY:

This week, we welcome three new companies to the Medical Supplies Industry in our Investment Survey: **Natus Medical Inc.**, **Masimo Corp.**, *and* **Volcano Corp.**, *on pages 216, 211, and 231, respectively.*

Timely **Wright Medical** *shares (page 233) stand out as a solid investment, given that the company's orthopedic products are in growing demand from a baby-boom generation that insists on prolonging its active lifestyle.*

Top-ranked **C.R. Bard** *stock (page 178) is an attractive option during this period of economic misery, thanks to its non-cyclical nature and strong earnings potential.*

Stryker Corp. *shares are an appealing choice for both the near term and long haul, partly due to strong finances which position Stryker well when consummating acquisitions at deeply discounted prices. See our report on page 228.*

Becton Dickinson *stock (page 181) exhibits potent long-term rebound potential in comparison with its historical averages. This is an opportunity that shouldn't be passed up given the equity's excellent credentials (top-ranked for both Safety and Timeliness).*

Tollgrade *shares may be of interest to the venturesome, given the likely prospect of a higher bid by an avid suitor. See our take on its future on page 142.*

★★ Rank 1 (Highest) for Timeliness.
★ Rank 2 (Above Average).

In three parts: Part 1 is the Summary & Index. Part 2 is Selection & Opinion. This is Part 3, Ratings & Reports. Volume LXIV, No. 27

Published weekly by VALUE LINE PUBLISHING, INC. 220 East 42nd Street, New York, NY 10017-5891

Wall Street Journal (http://online.wsj.com/home-page).
  Published by Dow Jones and Company, a key source of data and analysis
  regarding the securities markets, Dow Jones averages and other indices,
  daily stock charts for each exchange, and special features: "Heard on
  the Street," "Market Beat," Investment Advice." The *Wall Street Journal*
  is accessible also through ProQuest Direct (with the Wall Street Journal
  and Wall Street Journal Historical databases).

Wharton Research Data Service (WRDS) (http://wrds.wharton.upenn.edu).
  Intended for research purposes only, WRDS is an economic and financial
  data management system. Subscribers include universities and
  government institutions. Included with the WRDS subscription are
  access to databases—the ones relevant to stock market–related
  research are the CBOE (Chicago Board Options Exchange), Dow Jones,
  Philadelphia Stock Exchange, SEC Disclosure of Order Execution,
  CAPITAL IQ (COMPUSTAT), CRSP, CSMAR, IBES, Institute for the
  Study of Security Markets (ISSM), NASTRAQ, NYSE Euronext, and
  Thomson Reuters.

LOCATING DATA ON OBSOLETE SECURITIES

Directory of Obsolete Securities: Annual Guide to Stocks. Jersey City, NJ: Financial
  Information, Inc. Annual, 1970– (http:///www.fiinet.com).
  Listings of obsolete, discontinued securities include explanations of
  what had happened to the stock (change of name, bankruptcy, merger,
  acquisition, dissolution, or reorganization). Lists the value of the
  stock at the time of merger or acquisition. Also indicated is the year the
  securities became obsolete and whether the stock still has any financial
  value.

STOCK MARKET HISTORY

In addition to the reference resource listed, the stock exchanges generally feature a chronology and history. For example, the NYSE's
website has a chronology, accessible by selecting "About Us" and
then the subcategory "History." The NYSE's chronology is from
1653 to the present. Additionally, there are books about the major
exchanges and the stock market, most notably those by Robert Sobel
and Charles R. Geisst.

Wyckoff, Peter. *Wall Street and the Stock Markets: A Chronology, 1644–1971.*
  Philadelphia: Chilton Book Co., 1972.
  This reference guide to the history of the stock market is divided into four
  parts: "A Chronology (1644–1971)," Historical Records," The Averages,"

and "Market Influences." Part 1 is a chronology of key events of 1644, when a notice was posted that located Wall Street; May 17, 1792, the day of the signing of the Buttonwood Tree Agreement; and the stock market crash of 1929. Part 2, "Historical Records," contains statistics, including NYSE seat (membership) prices; daily volumes on the AMEX and the NYSE. Part 3, "The Averages," includes historical records of Dow Jones and other leading averages. Part 4, "Market Influences," chronicles the effects of major historical events (e.g., President Lincoln's assassination) and the effects on the market, theories and the market (e.g., the Dow theory), and a glossary of terms.

REGULATORY ISSUES

A key concern throughout the history of the securities markets has been the protection of investors. Prior to the stock market crash of 1929, investors were subject to false claims regarding their prospective investments, and there were no disclosure requirements. The SEC reports, "During the 1920s, approximately 20 million large and small shareholders took advantage of post-war prosperity and set out to make their fortunes in the stock market. It is estimated that of the $50 billion in new securities offered during this period, half became worthless" (http://www.sec.gov/about/whatwedo.shtml). When the stock market crashed at the end of the 1920s, investors lost large sums of money and many their entire fortunes. At this point, to investigate the markets, Congress held hearings to examine reasons for the market failure and recommend improvements. As a result, two key laws were passed: the Securities Act of 1933 and the Securities Exchange Act of 1934, the latter law creating the SEC. As a result of this legislation, full disclosure to investors became required by law with information about the company selling securities as well as facts about the risks involved in investing in these securities. The legislation also required brokers to put the investors first and be honest in their dealings with them.

Over the next few decades, other legislation went into effect, including the Investment Company Act of 1940, the Investment Advisors Act of 1940, and the Sarbanes-Oxley Act of 2002, the latter putting into effect reforms including enhancement of financial disclosure practices and creating the Public Company Account Oversight Board, which oversees activities of the auditing profession.

The SEC (http://www.sec.gov) was established in 1934, and its first chairman was Joseph P. Kennedy. The SEC was given the authority to register, regulate, and oversee brokerage firms, transfer agencies, and self-regulatory organizations (SROs). SROs are the stock exchanges themselves, including the NYSE and AMEX. The SEC is organized in several divisions: Corporate Finance (overseeing corporate disclosure practices), Trading and Markets (works to maintain fair, orderly, and efficient markets), Investment Management (responsible for investor protection), and Enforcement (recommends investigations of securities law violations.

The full texts of various legislation related to the securities markets are found on the SEC's website. The SEC also contains information on its website on litigation, proposed rules, and administrative proceedings and a form for investors to report complaints about broker or firm misconduct and investment email spam.

OTHER LEGAL RESOURCES

Commerce Clearing House. *Federal Securities Law Reporter*. Frederick, MD: Wolters Kluwer/Aspen Publishers. Loose-leaf service.
    Covers federal laws and rules regulating the issuance of securities, corporate disclosure, broker-dealer requirements, insider reporting, and investment companies. Provides full text of all federal securities laws, SEC regulations and forms, full text of federal securities law, SEC releases, and SEC no-action letters.

Commerce Clearing House, *Federal Securities Regulation Integrated Library* (Wolters Kluwer/CCH Aspen Publishers) (http://www.wksecurities.com).
    Online resource for securities resource practitioners and researchers. Contains primary and secondary sources and current news. Contains Current Developments (official releases and updates from 13 securities regulatory agencies and the text of the Commerce Clearing House's *Federal Securities Law Report Letter*), Source Materials (*Federal Securities Law Reporter, SEC Docket, SEC Enforcement Actions, Federal Securities Cases Archive, SEC Compliance and Disclosure Interpretations, SEC-No-Action Letters*, and *SEC Staff Comments Letters*), and Treatises/Analytical Material (*U.S. Regulation of the International Securities and Derivative Markets, SEC Rules and Explanation, Corporate Finance and the Securities Laws, Securities Regulation in Cyberspace*, and *Regulation of Securities: SEC Answer Book*).

Commerce Clearing House. *NYSE/AMEX Guide*. Frederick, MD: Wolters Kluwer/Aspen Publishers. Online and print formats.
    Formerly the *American Stock Exchange Guide*, contains rules of the NYSE/ AMEX.

Commerce Clearing House. *New York Stock Exchange Guide*. Frederick, MD: Wolters Kluwer/Aspen Publishers. Online, print, and CD-ROM formats.
    Contains directory of NYSE officers, members, and member organizations and full-text of bylaws and rules of the exchange.

PERIODICAL INDEXES AND FULL-TEXT DATABASES

Recommended to locate market trends are ABI/INFORM, Business Source Premier, Wilson Business databases, and ScienceDirect. To search for information on stock market history, recommended databases are, *Wall Street Journal*, (ProQuest) and *JSTOR*.

PERIODICALS AND NEWSPAPERS

Barron's (http://www.barrons.com)
Bloomberg Businessweek (http://www.businessweek.com)
Forbes (http://www.forbes.com)
Fortune (http://money.cnn.com/magazines/fortune)
Institutional Investor (http://www.imagazine.com)
Journal of Finance (http://www.afa.job.org)
Penny Stocks Magazine (http://www.pennystocksmagazine.com)
The Stock Market Journal (http://www.thestockmarketjournal.com)
Wall Street Journal (http://online.wsj.com/home-page)

6

Investing in Bonds, Mutual Funds, and Exchange-Traded Funds

BONDS

Bonds are defined as "any interest bearing or discounted government or corporate security that obliges the issuer to pay the bondholder a specified sum of money, usually at specific intervals and to pay the principal amount of the loan at maturity" (*Dictionary of Finance and Investment Terms*, p. 59). There are several types of bonds: corporate bonds (i.e., debt instruments issued by a company), U.S. government securities, and municipal bonds. Corporate bonds and U.S. government securities include Treasury bills, notes, and bonds. Municipal bonds are issued by towns, cities, and regional and local agencies. Investors looking to buy bonds look to ratings measuring the creditworthiness of the bond issuer. Rating agencies include Mergent, Standard & Poor's, and Fitch, and "grades" of bonds range from AAA (the highest) and D (the lowest). Bonds rated below B are termed "junk bonds." The chart below illustrates the ratings system.

Long Term Bond Rating Comparisons: Standard & Poor's and Moody's

Investment Grade	Standard & Poor's	Moody's
Highest Quality	AAA	Aaa
High Quality. High Grade	AA+, AA, AA-	Aa1, Aa3, Aa3
Upper Medium Grade	A, A, A-	A1, A2, A3
Lower Medium Grade	BBB+, BBB, BBB-	Baa1,Baa2, Baa3

Speculative, Non-investment Grade		
Non-investment Grade	BB+	Ba1
Speculative	BB, BB-	Ba2, Ba3
Highly Speculative	B+, B, B-	B1, B2, B3
Substantial Risk	CCC+	Caa1
Poor	CCC, CCC-	Caa2, Caa3
Default	D	-

Encyclopedias and Dictionaries

Downes, John. *Dictionary of Finance and Investment Terms*. 8th ed. Hauppauge, N.Y.: Barron's Educational Series, 2010.
  Defines terms on finance and investing, including those related to bonds. Definitions include baby bond, bond rating, bond swap, and bond discount.

Investopedia—Bond Terms (http://www.investopedia.com/categories/bonds.asp).
  A-to-Z list of definitions related to bonds with cross-references and links to related sites. Also features the sections "The Basics of Municipal Bonds" and "Corporate Bonds: An Introduction to Credit Risk."

Peterson, Nora. *Wall Street Lingo: Thousands of Investment Terms Explained Simply*. Ocala, FL: Orlando Publishing Group, 2007.
  Includes definitions of bond-related terms, including bond calendar, B rating, call date, bond swap, and face value.

Guides

AAA Rated: Unscrambling the Bond Market. Sponsored by the RUSA Business Reference and Services Section (BRASS). Edited by Lydia E. LaFaro. RUSA Occasional Papers, Number 22. Chicago: Reference and User Services Association, 1997.
  Papers from a BRASS Program presented at the American Library Association annual conference, July 8, 1996, with an introduction by Lydia E. LaFaro. Speaker presentations: bonds and the bond market by Louise Klusek, bond ratings by Steven L. Lubetkin, and sources of bond information by Louise Klusek. A bibliography of bond information sources is presented by Louise Klusek, a listing of major bond indexes by Gary White and Craig Wilkins, and a glossary of bond terms by Gary White, Tom Mirkovich, and Craig Wilkins. Klusek's paper "Bonds and the Bond Market" introduces the bond market, defining terms and types of bonds,

with a bibliography; Lubetkin's paper focuses on bond ratings, describing their origins and discussing rating categories. Klusek's second paper, "Sources of Bond Information," discusses bond issues, bond rating agencies, and other sources.

Thau, Annette. *The Bond Book: Everything Investors Need to Know about Treasuries, Municipals, GNMAs, Corporates, Zeros, Bond Funds, Money Market Funds, and More.* 3rd ed. New York: McGraw-Hill, 2010.
Guide to investors for both inexperienced and seasoned bond investors. Provides how-to information and practical advice on investing. Provides listing of online resources related to the bond markets. Covers buying individual bonds or bond funds, rating scales for bonds, the safest investments, junk bonds, and municipal bonds.

Wild, Russell. *Bond Investing for Dummies.* Hoboken, NJ: Wiley, 2007.
Explains the pros and cons of investment in bonds and offers advice on buying and selling bonds and bond funds, measuring risks and returns, taxation considerations, customizing and optimizing the portfolio, common bond investing mistakes and how to avoid them, and how to invest in tax-free municipal bonds, Treasury bonds, and high-yield corporate bonds.

How to Find Bond Statistics and Ratings

Barron's Market Lab (http://online.barrons.com/mktlab#mod=BOL_hpp _tools_market_lab).
Contains data on statistics including U.S. Treasury securities, Dow Jones corporate bond averages, weekly bond statistics, bond volume, NYSE bond index, Value Line convertible indexes, the most active corporate bonds, and bond rating changes.

Bloomberg Professional (http://www.bloomberg.com/professional)
Contains data files related to the bond markets including municipals, corporate bonds, and fixed issue markets.

The Bond Buyer (http://www.bondbuyer.com). Print and online editions.
Focuses on municipal bonds and features current new reports, the week's top five issues, municipal bond issue update, competitive bond new issue calendar, real-time pricing, the 500 largest municipal portfolios at U.S. banks, and the 100 largest institutional holders of municipal bonds.

BondsOnline (http://www.bondsonline.com).
Features links to newsletters, the day's market statistics/charts, a glossary of trading terms, a quote center, and investor tools. The BondsOnline Advisor features income security regulations.

Federal Reserve Statistical Release (http://www.federalreserve.gov/releases/ h15/data.htm).
Provides daily interest rates for selected U.S. Treasury and private money market and capital market instruments. Updated weekly and includes up to 30 years of historical data on selected items.

Financial Industry Regulatory Authority: Bonds (http://cxa.marketwatch
.com/finra/BondCenter/Default.aspx).
  Contains general bond market information, including news reports; a
  benchmark yields section; corporate bond market activity and performance information; data on U.S. Treasury, agency, corporate, and municipal bonds; credit rating information from the major rating agencies; and
  price information with real-time transaction prices for corporate and
  agency bonds (TRACE) and municipal bonds (MSRB) and end-of-day
  prices for U.S. Treasury bonds. Provides a "Bond Yield and Performance
  at a Glance" chart, FINRA TRACE Corporate Bond Market Activity, and
  FINRA-Bloomberg Most Active U.S. Corporate Bonds Indices. Includes
  a guide for investors, "Smart Bond Investing," featuring a glossary and
  guides on how to invest and buy and sell bonds.

Financial Times (London) (http://www.ft.com/home/us). Print and online
  formats.
  In addition to articles about the bond markets, contains data on bonds—
  global investment grade, bonds—benchmark government, bonds—index-
  linked, bonds—10-year government spreads, bond indices, bond—high
  yields and emerging market, U.S. yield curve, and bonds—government
  spreads.

Fitch Ratings (http://www.fitchratings.com/index_fitchratings.cfm).
  "A leading global rating agency committed to providing the world's credit
  markets with independent, timely and prospective credit opinions"
  (website). Website contains reports including "Ratings Process" and "
  U.S. Corporate Bond Market: A Review of Third-Quarter 2010 Ratings
  and Issuance Activity." The Fitch Research Tool Bond Compare allows
  users to compare structured finance bond performance data.

Investinginbonds.com (http://www.investinginbonds.com).
  A practical guide to investing in bonds with features including "Bond
  Basics," "What You Should Know," "Buying and Selling Bonds," "Types
  of Bonds," and "Bonds at Your Stage of Life." Also provides data on the
  most active bonds, recent trades, and statistics on specific issuers.

Mergent Bond Record (http://www.mergent.com). Print and online formats).
  Online edition: The Mergent Bond Viewer covers U.S. taxable and municipal bonds and provides issue details, including company description,
  offer amount, CUSIP, and industry code; historical pricing; current and
  historical ratings; coupon details; and corporate actions or significant
  events at the issuer level. Print edition: *Mergent Bond Record*, issued
  monthly, covers corporates, convertibles, governments, and municipals
  and features global ratings.

Monthly Statement of the Public Debt of the United States (Treasury Direct) (http://
  www.treasurydirect.gov/govt/reports/pd/mspd/mspd.htm).
  Features data on savings bond issues, redemptions, and maturity by series,
  securities issued in Treasury Direct, and U.S. savings bonds and notes.

NYSE Bonds (http://www.nyse.com/bonds/nysebonds/1095449059236.html). The NYSE operates the largest centralized bond market of any U.S. exchange, covering corporate, agency, and government bonds. The NYSE Euronext Market in Europe offers bond trading. The Bond Web Book allows searching of the bond market by CUSIP number or NYSE Symbol.

Standard & Poor's Credit Week (http://sandp.ecnext.com/coms2/page_credit week). Available in print and PDF formats, published 48 times per year.
Contains special reports (focus on topics in market); cover stories, articles, and a credit spotlight (features articles by senior analysts with in-depth examination of current industry, regulatory, and market trends and breaking news and developments in the global capital markets for issuers and their credit ratings), ratings trends charts (ratings/actions, new issuance volume, and pricing trends and secondary market yields and spreads for investment-grade and high-yield corporate bonds tracked and analyzed by Standard & Poor's Global Fixed Income Research Group), and the Sovereign Ratings List (local currency and foreign exchange ratings and outlooks).

Standard & Poor's NetAdvantage Bond Screener (http://www.netadvantage .standardandpoors.com/NASApp/NetAdvantage/index.do).
Searchable database by industry, company, and CUSIP. For each bond, data include ticker, issue, rating, maturity date, industry, 52-week low price, 52-week high price, sales price, and current yield.

Treasury Direct (http://www.treasurydirect.gov).
Includes instructions and information about the purchase of Treasury bills (short-term government securities with maturities ranging from a few days to 52 weeks), Treasury notes (government securities issued with maturities of 2, 3, 5, 7, and 10 years that pay interest every six months), Treasury bonds (pay interest every six months and mature in 30 years), Treasury inflation-protected securities (marketable securities whose principal is adjusted by changes in the consumer price index and that pay interest every six months and are issued with maturities of 5, 10, and 30 years), savings bonds (low-risk savings product sold at face value that earn interest and protect consumers from inflation), and EE/E savings bonds (sold at one-half face value)

Value Line Convertibles Survey (http://www.valueline.com/Convertibles/)
Presents data and ratings for convertible bonds and includes definitions of terms and advice on investing in this market. Ranks approximately 600 issues with analysis and makes recommendations whether to buy or sell. Features a "Convertible Screener" enabling users to search for and evaluate convertibles based on factors of rank, investment grade, conversion premium, call/put dates, maturity date and industry.

Wall Street Journal. Market Data Center—Bonds, Rates, and Credit Markets (http://online.wsj.com/mdc/public/page/mdc_bonds.html?mod=mdc _topnav_2_3000).

Presents data for Treasuries, futures, bond indicators, quotes and trading statistics, global government bonds, bond and index benchmarks, bond offering calendar, corporate bonds—most active, and Treasury quotes.

Yahoo! Finance: Bonds Center (http://finance.yahoo.com/bonds).
Features bond statistics including a U.S. Treasury bond rates and bonds market summary plus a bonds primer, types of bonds, bond strategies, and a bond glossary.

PERIODICAL INDEXES AND FULL TEXT DATABASES

The databases *ABI/INFORM*, *Business Source Premier*, and *Dow Jones Factiva* all contain articles related to investments in bonds.

Dow Jones Factiva (http://factiva.com).
Contains aggregated news and information from over 17,000 global sources plus articles from the *Wall Street Journal*.

PERIODICALS

Barron's (http://online.barrons.com/home-page)
The Bond Buyer (http://www.bondbuyer.com)
BondWeek (http://www.aboutus.org/BondWeek.com)
Journal of Fixed Income (http://www.iijournals.com/toc/jfi/current)
Wall Street Journal (http://www.wsj.com)

MUTUAL FUNDS AND EXCHANGE-TRADED FUNDS

A mutual fund, operated by an investment company or fund manager, pools money contributed by investors, and the manager/company invests this money in a variety of investments (stocks, bonds, and so on). A mutual fund enables investors to have a diversified portfolio of investments.

An exchange-traded fund (ETF) is defined as "a form of mutual fund that trades on an exchange ... which invests in diversified securities based on market interest" (*The Complete Investment and Finance Dictionary*). The first ETF was introduced in 1993 at the American Stock Exchange.

Guides

Benz, Christine. *Morningstar Guide to Mutual Funds: Five-Star Strategies*. 2nd ed. Hoboken, NJ: Wiley, 2007.
Benz, director of mutual fund analysis at Morningstar, authored this practical guide to mutual funds, describing the latest research tools for

making investment decisions. Includes advice on how to build a portfolio of funds, how to review and track the fund, and how to assess the quality of a mutual fund's manager.

Investopedia, *Mutual Funds: An Introduction* (http://www.investopedia .com/university/mutualfunds).
Guide to how to invest.

Kimmel, Russel. *Fund Spy: Morningstar's Inside Secrets to Selecting Mutual Funds That Outperform*. Hoboken, NJ: Wiley, 2009.
Kimmel, a Morningstar fund analyst, offers advice to investors on how to select the right funds for their portfolios. He offers advice on finding managers, studying the fund's performance, and how to screen and study a fund to decide on whether to purchase it.

Tyson, Eric. *Mutual Funds for Dummies*. 6th ed. Hoboken, NJ: Wiley, 2010.
Features tips on hiring a financial adviser, the top 10 fund investing mistakes and how to avoid them, buying funds from the best firms, tax considerations, how to evaluate funds and adjust the portfolio, how to work with mutual fund research tools, and sample portfolios.

Mutual Funds and ETF SOURCES

Barron's Market Data Center: Mutual Funds and ETFs (http://online.barrons .com/funds?mod=bol_mdc_topnav_9_3000).
In addition to news reports and analysis, contains a searchable database of mutual funds to locate their data, rankings, major holdings, distributions, and interactive charting. Also includes Fund Scope, a table showing performance of mutual funds selected by the editors; Fund Screener, allowing searching for funds by criteria including performance, feeds, asset allocation, and so on; and Fund & Stock Tables with weekly listings for stocks and funds on the NYSE, AMEX, and NASDAQ.

Bloomberg BusinessWeek Mutual Fund Scoreboard (http://www.business week.com/mutual_fund).
The Scoreboard is a tool updated each month to show performance of mutual funds. Listings may be browsed or searched by fund name or ticker symbol. Each fund listed contains name, fund type, *Bloomberg Businessweek* rating, assets, assets change percentage, expense ration, and pretax returns (by time periods 1 month ranging to 10 years).

Investment Company Institute (ICI) (http://www.ici.org).
The ICI is the "national association of U.S. investment companies, including mutual funds, closed-end funds, exchange-traded funds (ETFs) and unit investment trusts" (website). Features full text of "Research Commentary," a series of reports on various topics among which are "Competition in the Mutual Fund Business" and "Trends in the Fees and Expenses of Mutual Funds."

Lipper Mutual Fund Ratings (Thomson Research) (http://www.lipperweb.com).
   Lipper, a division of Thomson Research, is "a global leader in supplying
   mutual fund information, analytical tools, and commentary." Provides
   benchmarking, ratings, and classifications for asset managers throughout
   the world. Products include fact sheets and Fundfile (which tracks
   mutual funds data) and prepares custom market intelligence reports.

Mergent Online (http://www.mergent.com/productsServices-desktop
   Applications-online.html).
   Equity research reports section includes coverage of mutual fund data.

Morningstar Investment Research Center (http://library.morningstar.com/
   default.html).
   Contains Screen for Funds and Screen for ETFs for Funds: financial data on
   thousands of funds. Features fund picks, fund analyst reports, fund compare, most similar funds, international funds, and funds summary. For
   ETFs, financial data for hundreds of funds with current data on returns,
   reports, and Morningstar ratings. Also features ETFs by trading volume,
   ETF Analyst Reports, and ETF Valuation Quickrank.

Morningstar Mutual Funds Online (http://mfb.morningstar.com).
   Provides fund reports in PDF format. Covers domestic equity,
   international equity, taxable bonds, and municipal bonds. Each report
   provides name of fund, contact information (address, telephone, and
   website), and its goals, strategy, portfolio analysis, current investment
   data, Morningstar analysis, rating and risk, credit analysis, and performance. Subscribers can create a list of favorite funds and retrieve up-to-
   date reports of these funds.

Mutual Fund Investor's Center (http://www.mfea.com).
   "The Mutual Fund Education Alliance is a national trade association of
   mutual fund companies that offer funds direct., through supermarkets
   or through third parties and financial advisors" (website). Features
   "Investing Basics," providing advice on allocating assets and retirement,
   investment strategies, market commentary, top five funds by category,
   and links to information regarding buying from an online broker.

Standard & Poor's Mutual Fund Reports (http://www.netadvantage.standard
   andpoors.com/NetAd/MutualFund_Guide.pdf).
   For each report, data include name, highlights (recent developments and
   changes), fees and expenses, minimum investment required, recent trading data, overall category ranking determined by how one fund compares to another fund in same category, overall Standard & Poor's
   rating, and total return overview and tax analysis.

Value Line ETF Survey (http://www.valueline.com/Products/ETF_Products/
   The_Value_Line_ETF_Survey.aspx).
   Contains in-depth research of ETFs listed in the United States and Japan.
   Includes Value Line's proprietary ranking system, performance data,
   and Global Heat Maps to locate holdings in specific countries and regions
   with weekly updates on new ETF launches.

Wall Street Journal Market Research Center, Mutual Funds and ETFs (http://
online.wsj.com/public/page/etf-mutual-funds.html).
  Contains Market Screener, a source of data for ETFs (actives, gainers, and
  decliners daily closing prices by exchange, daily closing prices by sponsor, and ETF Screener) and mutual funds (closed-end funds by category,
  closing prices of mutual funds, Fund Screener, mutual fund yardsticks,
  Lipper indexes, mutual fund yardsticks, and money market funds). Also
  features an introductory guide to investing plus articles and analysis on
  mutual funds and ETFs.

Yahoo! Finance: Mutual Funds Center (http://finance.yahoo.com/funds).
  Features mutual fund news, Fund Screener, top performers, Morningstar
  editorials, Mutual Funds 101, mutual fund basics, how to choose a fund,
  tax issues, and interactive videos.

PERIODICAL INDEXES AND FULL-TEXT DATABASES

Articles in journals/newspapers may be located by searching the
databases *ABI/INFORM, Business Source Premier,* and *Wall Street Journal*
(ProQuest).

PERIODICALS

Barron's (http://www.barrons.com)
Morningstar Fund Investor (http://mfi.morningstar.com/purchase.aspx)
Wall Street Journal (http://www.wsj.com)

7

Commodities, Options, Futures, Derivatives, and Hedge Funds

COMMODITIES

Commodities are products that include those in the "soft" category, including grain, cocoa, coffee, orange juice, sugar, and pork bellies, and those in the "hard" category, among which are metals, chemicals, and oil. Trades take place within commodity exchanges. It should be noted that futures and options do involve the trading of commodities.

Encyclopedias and Dictionaries

Erickson, Rosemary, and George Steinbeck. *The Language of Commodities: A Commodity Glossary.* New York: New York Institute of Finance, 1985.
  Dictionary of terms, among which are gold reserve, premium market value, commodity, commodity price index, commodity rate, index, and futures market. Also features the sections "How to Read the Commodity Financial Quotes," "Basic Calculations," and "How to Find a Commodity Factor" and Reference Guides (e.g., trading markets and related organizations).

Investopedia (http://www.investopedia.com).
  Provides definitions of terms for investors in commodities, select dictionaries, and search for commodity-related terms.

Guides

Bouchentouf, Amine. *Commodities for Dummies.* New York: Wiley, 2006

Covers topics including how to invest, how commodities compare to other investments, research methods for analyzing commodities, and how commodities stack up against other investment vehicles.

Garner, Carley. *A Trader's First Book on Commodities: An Introduction to the World's Fastest Growing Markets.* Upper Saddle River, NJ: Pearson Education, FT Press, 2010.
Written by a commodity broker and analyst, this source contains practical advice about commodities investing and includes explanations of terms and methods of investing.

Data and Statistics Sources

The following research sources include the specific commodity exchanges, government agencies, periodical publications, and reference sources from commercial publishers.

ABI INFORM Commodity Reports (http://www.proquest.com/en-US).
Quarterly reports from the EIU Economist Intelligence Unit provide insight into how emerging markets, driven by commodities, affect the global economy. Reports cover foods, feedstuff, beverages, and industrial raw materials.

Barron's (http://online.barrons.com/mktlab).
Features data on the Commodity Futures Index and information on gold prices and trading.

Bloomberg Commodity Futures (http://www.bloomberg.com/markets/commodities/futures)
Features Commodity Futures Index data and trading data for specific commodities within the categories of agriculture, energy, livestock, and metals.

Bloomberg Professional –Commodities (http://www.bloomberg.com/professional/commodities/
Provides pricing and statistical data for commodities with current and historical data; the Bloomberg Commodities Toolbox which features calculators that help price commodity swaps and options among other data; and BMAP a tool that helps spot "potential price movements by integrating physical assets with severe weather analysis."

CNN Money.com Commodities (http://money.cnn.com/data/commodities).
Provides news releases in addition to trading data for specific commodities in the categories of energy, agriculture, and metals, meat and livestock, and consumer (e.g., cocoa and coffee). Includes 52-week price range for each commodity.

CPM Group (http://www.cpmgroup.com/main.php).
The CPM Group is a commodities market research, consulting, asset management, and investment-banking firm. Features publications for sale,

among which are *CPM Gold Yearbook*, *CPM Silver Yearbook*, *CPM Platinum Group Metals Yearbook*, and *CPM Weekly (Commodity Views)*.

CRB Commodity Yearbook. Commodity Research Bureau (http://www.crbtrader .com). Hoboken, NJ: Wiley. Annual.
  Features the Commodity Price Trend, a review of the CCI Index and analyses of performance of commodities: energy, grains, industrials, livestock, precious metals, and softs (i.e., cocoa, coffee, orange juice, and sugar); tables and charts of CRB indices; U.S. futures volume highlights; exchange data from the Chicago Board of Trade, the Chicago Mercantile Exchange, ICE, and the New York Mercantile Exchange; options traded; and analyses and date of specific commodities, among which are aluminum, cement, cocoa, coffee, copper, cotton, currencies, gasoline, gold, heating oil, lumber and plywood, pork bellies, soybean oil, peanuts and peanut oil, oranges and orange juice, tallow and greases, and tobacco. Also contains section on stock index futures.

Chicago Mercantile Exchange (CME) (http://www.cmegroup.com).
  The CME's stated purpose is to serve "the risk management needs of customers around the globe" (website). The exchange provides range of benchmark futures and options products available on any exchange covering asset classes of commodities, equities, interest rates, and so on. Features the *CME Group* magazine, available online; this periodical includes articles on outlook for interest rates, articles on specific commodities, and outlook for international currencies. Presents trading data on commodities representing agricultural products, energy, and metals. It should be noted that the Chicago Board of Trade (since 2007) and the New York Mercantile Exchange (since 2008) are now part of the CME Group.

Commodity Floor Brokers and Traders Association (http://www.cfbta.org).
  Nonprofit group representing the interests of the New York trading community. Provides links to resources (among which are exchanges) related to commodity trading.

FAO Stat (Food and Agriculture Organization of the United Nations (http:// faostat.fao.org).
  Features time-series and cross-sectional data for food and agriculture in approximately 200 countries with production figures for each country of livestock and crops. Contains a chart on the top 20 commodities and producers. Contains a food balance sheet with data on a country's food supply and for each type of commodity available for human consumption. The supply utilization accounts, which are time-series data with statistics on supply (production, imports, and stock changes) and utilization (exports, feed and seek, and food), allow correlation of food availability with food use. Features link to International Commodity Prices (http:// www.fao.org/es/esc/prices/PricesServlet.jsp?lang=en), which is a database organized by specific commodities and allowing searching (by year and country) for items including bananas, beef, cotton, soybeans, wool, and tapioca.

HardAssetsInvestor.com (http://www.hardassetsinvestor.com).
   Provides research-oriented focus for investors wanting to learn about commodity investing, commodity futures, and gold. Features data on "hard commodities," investment advice, articles, a video library, and "Hard Assets University," a course for current and potential investors. Links to resources are provided in the "University" section.

Kansas City Board of Trade (http://www.kcbt.com).
   Commodity futures and options exchange specializing in wheat. Features data for wheat market analysis and outlook, wheat trading volume, deliverable wheat stocks, and wheat deliveries.

Minneapolis Grain Exchange (MGEX) (http://www.mgex.com).
   The MGEX offers index-based contracts to hard red spring wheat contracts. Additionally, index futures and options contracts are offered on hard red spring wheat, hard red winter wheat, soft red winter wheat, corn, and soybeans. Includes index futures quotes for these specific commodity products.

TFC Commodity Charts (http://tfc-charts.w2d.com).
   Contains charts for commodity futures trading including charts for specific commodities and provides researchers with tools to create their own charts based on various parameters. Also includes link to commodity brokers and a glossary of terms.

Thomson Reuters/Jeffries CRB Index (http://thomsonreuters.com/products_services/financial/thomson_reuters_indices/indices/commodity_indices).
   Online database for specific commodity equity indices: Global Energy Equity Index, Global Agriculture Equity, Global Industrial Metals Equity Index, Global Precious Metals Equity Index, and R/J CRB Global Commodity Equity Index (CRBQX).

U.S. Commodity Futures Trading Commission (CFTC) (http://www.cftc.gov).
   The CFTC was created in 1974 by Congress to act as an independent agency with the mandate to regulate commodity futures and options markets in the United States. Provides information on law and regulation. The Market Reports feature the following sections: Commitments of Traders (a breakdown of each Tuesday's open interest for markets in which 20 or more traders hold positions equal to or above the reporting events established by the CFTC), Financial Data for Futures Commission Merchants or FCMs, This Month in Futures Markets, Bank Participation Report, Index Investment Data, Cotton On-Call, and Futures Industry Registrants by Location.

U.S. Department of Agriculture, National Agricultural Statistics Service (http://www.nass.usda.gov).
   The National Agricultural Statistics Service "provides timely, accurate, and useful statistics in service to U.S. agriculture" (website). Contains news reports and statistics for crops and plants and livestock and animals. A database allows searching by categories (e.g., for crops, narrow the search to fruit and tree nuts to obtain statistics for oranges). Statistics for oranges

yield data on production and price received for various categories of this product. Also provides access to specific reports on, among other topics, agricultural prices, cattle, crop production, grain stocks, hogs and pigs, rice stocks, prospective plantings, and crop progress (national). Features historical publications: Census of Agriculture, Agricultural Statistics, Track Records (crops, livestock, and grain stocks), Trends (20th Century), and Price Reactions (after crop or livestock reports).

U.S. Geological Survey, Commodity Statistics and Information, Minerals Information (http://minerals.usgs.gov/minerals/pubs/commodity).
 Search by specific mineral commodity for data and information. For example, for gold, a paragraph is included on its historical background and its uses; also included are links to related publications, Search year by year (from ca. 1996 to 2010) for statistics on production, price, imports and exports, consumption, world mine production and reserve, and substitutes. Also provides email addresses and phone numbers for mineral commodity specialists and links to relevant trade associations.

Wall Street Journal, Markets, Commodities (http://online.wsj.com/public/page/news-oil-gold-commodities.html).
 Features the latest commodities headlines (including news on specific commodities); market information, commodity futures and indices (for specific items, including crude oil, coffee, soybeans, and sugar), cash commodity prices, and complete commodity market data for specific items/products in agriculture, energy, interest, index metals, and lumber.

Yahoo! Finance—Commodities Futures (http://finance.yahoo.com/futures).
 Features market trading data and headline news information.

Associations Representing Specific Commodities

The following are representative examples of trade associations:

American Metal Market (http://www.amm.com)
American Petroleum Association (http://www.api.org)
American Soybean Association (http://www.soygrowers.com)
International Cocoa Organization (http://www.icco.org)
International Coffee Association (http://www.ico.org)
National Association of Wheat Growers (http://www.wheatworld.org)
National Cotton Council of America (http://www.cotton.org)
The Sugar Association (http://www.sugar.org)
World Gold Council (http://www.gold.org)

Regulatory Issues

Commerce Clearing House, *Commodities and Derivatives Integrated Library* (http://www.wksecurities.com). Frederick, MD: Walters Kluwer/CCH Aspen Publishers.

Online resource features full text of relevant laws, rules, and cases. Contains current developments (*Hedge Funds and Private Equity Regulation and Risk Management Update Newsletter, Commodity Futures Reporter Letters,* and *Derivatives Regulation Reporter Letters*), primary source materials (*Commodity Futures Law Reporter* and *Derivatives Regulation Law Reporter*), and treatise/analytical material (*Derivatives Regulation, U.S. Regulation of the Internationals Securities and Derivatives Markets, Securitization of Financial Assets,* and *Commodity Futures Modernization Act of 2000: Law and Explanation*).

Commerce Clearing House. *Commodity Futures Law Reporter.* Frederick, MD: Wolters Kluwer/Aspen Publishers. Online and print formats.
With biweekly updates, provides full text of laws and regulations, annotations of court cases, administrative decisions, relevant excerpts from the Congressional Committee Report, current development and trends, CFTF Staff Letters, and other relevant materials.

Periodical Indexes and Full-Text Databases

To search for articles on commodities, recommended databases are *ABI/INFORM, Business Source Premier,* and *ScienceDirect.*

Journals and Newspapers

Barron's (http://online.barrons.com/home-page)
Financial Times (http://online.barrons.com/home-page)
Journal of Banking and Finance (http://www.elsevier.com/wps/find/journaldescription.cws_home/505558/description#description)
Journal of Public Economics (http://www.elsevier.com/wps/find/journaldescription.cws_home/505578/description#description)
Review of Financial Economics (http://www.elsevier.com/wps/find/journaldescription.cws_home/620170/description#description)
Wall Street Journal (http://online.wsj.com/home-page)

OPTIONS

An option is a right of an investor to buy or sell a set amounts of a commodity, currency, or security at a specific time and at an "exercise," or set, price; however, when the specific time arrives for the investor to buy or sell, he or she is not obligated to buy or sell at the exercise price. The investor can decide not to execute the transaction if it turns out to be not a profitable venture. The option to buy is termed a "call option," and the option to sell is called a "put option." Specific markets and exchanges focus on options transactions.

Dictionary

Webber, Alan. *Dictionary of Futures and Options*. Chicago: Probus, 1994.
Dictionary of terms involved in both futures and options investing.

Guides

An Investor's Guide to Trading Options. New York: Lightbulb Press, 2004.
Explains the basics of investing and describes options strategies for investors. Explains terms used in options trading.

Williams, Michael S., and Amy Hoffman. *Fundamentals of the Options Market*. New York: McGraw-Hill, 2001.
Introductory guide describes types of options and investing strategies. Includes statistical charts and a glossary of terms.

Data and Statistics Sources

BATS U.S. Options Exchange (http://www.batsoptions.com).
Features data on market volume, the most active options, and news and announcements

Barron's Market Data Center Options (http://online.barrons.com/mktlab).
Contains a section on data regarding futures and options, including CBOE Market Report (put/call ratio and advances and declines, and so on) and stock index options.

Boston Options Exchange (BOX) (http://www.nyse.com/equities/nysearca equities/1156241406908.html).
Contains data on BOX trade volume, options classes listed, daily market share, and price improvement.

Chicago Board Options Exchange (http://www.cboe.com).
The CBOE was founded in 1973 as the first U.S. options exchange, and trading begins on standardized, listed options. Its website features trading statistics, CBOE Index charts, options-based benchmark indexes, LiveOptions real-time streaming quotes, history and time line of the CBOE, online tutorials, and publications available for purchase.

New York Stock Exchange AMEX Equities (http://www.nyse.com/equities/nysealternextus/1218155408912.html).
Provides a video clip explaining options market, news releases, and trading data.

New York Stock Exchange Arca (http://www.nyse.com/equities/nysearca equities/1156241406908.html).
The NYSE venue for options trading—features trading statistics and market organization details.

New York Stock Exchange, Arca Options (http://www.nyse.com/futures
options/nysearcaoptions/1151534050804.html).
   Provides data on trading, trader updates, options by equity symbol, and
   guides to trading.

Options Clearing Corporation (http://www.theocc.com).
   Provides statistics on daily volume by exchange and historical volume
   statistics.

Options Industry Council (http://www.optionseducation.org).
   An organization designed to educate investors and their financial advisers
   about the benefits of options trading. The website offers quotes, seminars
   and webcasts, and trading tools (links to guides, glossaries, and so on).

Value Line Daily Options Survey (http://www.valueline.com/Options). Print
and online editions.
   Provides interactive daily analysis and rankings of over 200,000 stock and
   stock index options. Features evaluations and rankings on both bid and
   ask prices (twice a day, noon, and at the close) and the Interactive Options
   and Online Options Screener, with access to Value Line analysis and recommendations for over 200,000 options. Subscription includes *The Weekly
   Option Strategist* (published 48 times per year).

Wharton Research Data Services (http://wrds.wharton.upenn.edu)
   WRDS is a Web-based business data research service from the Wharton
   School at the University of Pennsylvania, a research tool for academics.
   Contains the following databases related to options:

CBOE Chicago Board Options Exchange (http://www.cboe.com/)
   Volatility Index (VIX) key measure of market expectations of near-term
   volatility conveyed by S&P 500 stock index option prices. Measures
   market's expectation of 30-day volatility. VIX is based on S&P 500 index
   option prices and incorporates information from the volatility skew by
   using a wider range of strike prices rather than just at the money series.

International Securities Exchange (ISE) (http://www.ise.com).
   The first all-electronic options exchange in the United States, offers
   options trading on over 2,000 underlying equity, ETF, index, and FX
   products. Provides news releases, volume and share statistics, quotes,
   volatility, and a calculator. Also features an education center with a
   guide to the basics of options trading, podcasts, webinars, and investment strategies.

NasdaqTrader.com (NASDAQ OMX) (http://www.nasdaqtrader.com/
homepage.aspx).
   Provides options volume data for the Nasdaq Options Market and the
   Philadelphia Stock Exchange (which was acquired by the NASDAQ
   OMX).

Option Metrics Ivy DB (http://www.optionmetrics.com/ivydbus.html)
   A comprehensive source of historical price and implied volatility data
   for the U.S. equity and index options markets.

Periodical Indexes and Full-Text Databases

To search for articles on options, the databases *ABI/INFORM, Business Source Premier (EBSCOhost)*, and *ScienceDirect* are recommended.

Periodicals and Newspapers

Financial Times (London) (http://www.ft.com/home/us)
Journal of Banking and Finance (http://www.elsevier.com/wps/find/journaldescription.cws_home/505558/description#description)
Journal of Financial Markets (http://www.elsevier.com/wps/find/journaldescription.cws_home/600652/description#description)
Wall Street Journal (http://www.wsj.com)

FUTURES

Futures are contractual agreements to buy or sell set amounts of commodities, currencies, interest rates, or stock indexes at a specific price (settlement price) for a preset future time. The preset future date is called the delivery date or the settlement date. Specific markets concentrate on trading futures.

Dictionary

Steinbeck, George, and Rosemary Erickson. *The Futures Markets Dictionary.* New York: New York Institute of Finance, 1988.
  Contains definitions of terms with cross-references. Terms defined include futures market, futures contract, cross trading, blocked exchange, and covered option. Also features the sections "How to Read the Commodity Financial Quotes," "Basic Calculations," and "How to Find a Commodity Factor" and supplies a reference guide.

Guides

Bernstein, Jake. *How the Futures Markets Work.* 2nd ed. Englewood Cliffs, NJ Prentice Hall, 2000.
  A guide to the futures markets, explains terms and advises how to invest through choosing a broker and placing orders and how to research the markets.

Duarte, Joe. *Futures and Options for Dummies.* New York: Wiley, 2006.
  Provides advice and information on how to analyze the markets, execution of successful trades, direction of commodity futures, and interest rate futures and speculating with currencies.

Thomsett, Michael C. *Winning with Futures: The Smart Way to Recognize Opportunities, Calculate Risk, and Maximize Profits.* New York: AMACOM, 2009.
An introductory guide to investing in the futures market. The author
defines terms, explains how the futures market works, describes its origins, and explains indices used, how to read and analyze futures prices,
risk levels, order placement, and classifications of futures.

Data and Statistics Sources

For a list of information sources on commodity futures, see the section
"Commodities" in this chapter.

Chicago Mercantile Exchange Group (http://www.cmegroup.com).
"CME Group exchanges offer the widest range of global benchmark products across all major asset classes, including futures and options based on
interest rates, equity indexes, foreign exchange, energy, agricultural commodities, metals, weather and real estate" (website). Features trading
data for futures and options from COMEX Futures, COMEX Options,
NYMEX Futures, and NYMEX Options.

Futures Industry Association (http://www.futuresindustry.org).
Its mission "focuses on three primary areas—education, ethics and data"
(website). Contains futures and index data and statistics for currency,
equity, meat, metal, interest rate, energy, grain, food/fiber, cash, and
futures and index pricing.

ICE Futures, Formerly Board of Trade of the City of New York) (https://
www.theice.com/homepage.jhtml).
An intercontinental exchange that operates leading regulated exchanges,
trading platforms, and clearinghouses, serving global markets for agricultural, credit, currency, emissions, energy, and equity index markets.
The ICE operates three futures exchanges, including London-based ICE
Futures Europe, which hosts trading in half the world's crude and
refined oil futures contracts traded each day. ICE Futures U.S. and ICE
Futures Canada list agricultural, currency, and Russell Index futures
and options markets. ICE also provides trade execution, processing, and
clearing services for the over-the-counter energy and credit derivatives
markets. A component of the Russell 1000 and S&P 500 indexes, ICE
serves customers in more than 55 countries and is headquartered in
Atlanta, Georgia, with offices in New York, London, Chicago, Winnipeg,
Calgary, Houston, and Singapore.

National Futures Association (NFA) (http://www.nfa.futures.org).
The NFA is "the industry wide, self-regulatory organization for the U.S.
futures industry" (website). Features news releases, regulatory updates,
a guide to avoiding investment scams and fraud, an investment newsletter, and a book of regulations and bylaws.

Periodical Indexes And Full-Text Databases

Databases to search for futures articles include *ABI/INFORM, Business Source Premier (EBSCOhost)*, and *ScienceDirect*.

Periodicals and Newspapers

Financial Times (http://www.ft.com/home/uk)
Futures Industry (http://www.futuresindustry.org/futures-industry.asp)
Futures Magazine (http://www.futuresmag.com/Pages/default.aspx)
Journal of Futures Markets (http://onlinelibrary.wiley.com/journal/10.1002/(ISSN)1096-9934)
Wall Street Journal (http://www.wsj.com)

DERIVATIVES

Derivatives are financial instruments whose value is determined or derived from underlying assets, among which are stocks, bonds, currencies, commodities, interest rates, and currencies. Derivatives are traded through agreements or contracts between two or more parties, and an agreed-on price is set up in advance between or among said parties. Exchange-traded derivatives are traded through specialized exchanges and over-the-counter derivatives through the over-the-counter markets.

Types of derivatives include swaps, or the simultaneous buying or selling of a security, and futures, or forward, contracts, or when an investor and a second party agree to buy or sell specific amounts of interest rates, currencies, and so on at certain dates in the future for specific prices.

Encyclopedias and Dictionaries

Inglis-Taylor, Andrew. *The Dictionary of Derivatives. Finance and Capital Markets.* Basingstoke: Palgrave-Macmillan, 1995.
Defines terms related to derivatives with cross-references. For investors and for students of business.

Lynn, Guy. *A Dictionary of Derivatives and Financial Engineering.* Oakland, CA: Mason, 2007.
Defines terms and jargon related to derivatives, covering approximately 10,000 terms related to derivatives, options, risk management, and financial engineering.

Guides

Tools of the Trade: A Basic Guide to Financial Derivatives (Federal Reserve Bank of
    Boston) (http://www.bos.frb.org/education/pubs/toolsoft.pdf).
    Explains background of the derivative market, how to invest, and
    researching strategies.

Data and Statistics Sources

Bank for International Settlements Data on Exchange Traded Derivatives
    (http://www.bis.org/statistics/extderiv.htm).
    The main purpose of the exchange-traded derivatives section is to obtain
    information about size, structure, and development of futures and
    options markets. In conjunction with semiannual over-the-counter deriv-
    atives, statistics provide comprehensive monitoring of international
    financial market activity. The main purpose of the exchange-traded deriv-
    atives statistics is to obtain extensive information of the size, structure,
    and developments of the futures and options markets so as to comple-
    ment and reinforce other, more traditional sets of financial statistics com-
    piled by the BIS. In conjunction with the semiannual over-the-counter
    derivatives statistics, they provide a more comprehensive monitoring of
    international financial market activity. Contains data and tables for
    exchange derivatives: exchange traded by instrument and location,
    national amounts, and number of contracts.

Chicago Mercantile Exchange Group (http://www.cmegroup.com).
    This group is the world's leading and most diverse derivatives market-
    place. The company is comprised of four designated contract markets.
    Further information on each exchange's rules and product listings can
    be found by clicking on the links to CME, CBOT, NYMEX, and COMEX.
    The CME ClearPort trading facilities (https://services.cmegroup.com/
    cpc) provide clearing and settlement services for exchange-traded con-
    tracts and for over-the-counter derivatives transactions.

OTC QX (http://www.otcqx.com/otcqx).
    Presents data for over-the-counter traded derivatives in the United States
    and internationally.

TMX Group (http://www.tmx.com/en/about_tsx).
    TMX Group's businesses operate cash and derivative markets for
    multiple-asset classes, including equities, fixed income, and energy. Fea-
    tures trading data, an exchange blog, and a listed company directory.

Periodical Indexes and Full-text Databases

See under Futures.

Periodicals and Newspapers

Journal of Derivatives (http://www.iijournals.com/toc/jod/current)
Journal of Derivatives and Hedge Funds (http://www.palgrave-journals.com/
    jdhf/index.html)
Journal of Financial Economics (http://jfe.rochester.edu)
Wall Street Journal (http://www.wsj.com)

HEDGE FUNDS

A hedge fund consists of investment capital contributed by a relatively
small group of wealthy investors each of whom makes relatively large
contributions. It is generally organized as a limited partnership with
investment strategies that are more high risk, such as margin buying
and options strategies.

Dictionary

Investopedia Hedge Fund Dictionary (http://www.investopedia.com/
    investing-topics/Hedge_Funds/Term)
    Dictionary of terms and jargon used for hedge fund investing.

Guide

Logue, Ann C. *Hedge Funds for Dummies*. Hoboken, NJ: Wiley, 2006.
    Guide covers what a hedge fund is, its organization, how to invest, evalu-
    ating fund performance, tax issues, and strategies.

Data and Statistics Sources

Alternative Investment Management Association (http://www.aima.org).
    The hedge fund industry's "global, not-for-profit trade association with
    over 1200 corporate members (with over 5000 individual contracts) in
    more than 40 countries worldwide" (website). Contains links to educa-
    tional resources, a guide to sound practices, links to related websites,
    and a glossary and publishes the *AIMA Journal*.

Hedge Fund Association (https://www.thehfa.org).
    A trade association site that describes facts and figures about hedge funds,
    popular hedge fund investment strategies, and links to full-text articles
    and white papers related to hedge funds.

The Hedge Fund Journal, Rankings (http://www.thehedgefundjournal.com/
    rankings).
    Features rankings of the Europe 50 (Europe's 50 largest single managers
    ranked by assets under management), the U.S. 50 (the top 50 single
    manager's ranked by assets under management), the Asia 25 (the top 25
    single managers ranked by assets under management), and the Fund of
    Hedge Funds Global 50 (ranked by assets under management).

Morningstar Hedge Fund Database (http://corporate.morningstar.com/us/
    asp/subject.aspx?xmlfile=545.xml).
    Contains data on 8,000 funds available to both U.S. and international
    investors. Provides the Hedge Fund Investment Detail Report, featuring
    name, contact information, information on investment requirements
    and founding date, performance data on minimum investment needed,
    and monthly distribution of returns, and the Hedge Fund Summary
    Report, featuring name, contact information, inception date, investment
    strategy, distribution of monthly returns, and return/risk analysis.

Periodical Indexes and Full-text Databases

See under Futures.

Periodicals and Newspapers

Financial Times (London) (http://www.ft.com/home/uk)
The Hedge Fund Journal (http://www.thehedgefundjournal.com)
Hedge Funds Review (http://www.hedgefundsreview.com)
Institutional Investor (http://www.institutionalinvestor.com/DefaultReg.aspx)
Journal of Derivatives and Hedge Funds (http://www.palgrave-journals.com/
    jdhf/index.html)
Journal of Wealth Management (http://www.iijournals.com/toc/jwm/current)
Wall Street Journal (http://www.wsj.com)

8

Economics

Economics is defined as "a social science concerned chiefly with description and analysis of the production, distribution, and consumption of goods and services" (*Merriam Webster Dictionary*). Branches of economics include macroeconomics, which examines a national or world economy as a whole and studies statistics on inflation, unemployment, and industrial production, and microeconomics, which focuses in on specific sectors, among which are companies, industries, or households. Econometrics applies statistical measures to study the economy.

The state of the economy on a national or global level is a major focus of news reports and presidential speeches and is a central issue for governments. How to improve it is a major platform for political candidates, and its failure or success impacts total populations. The study of the economy is of importance not just for academics but also for all who wish to monitor the health of their investments, and it also determines ones way of life.

This chapter focuses on sources of economic information for the United States and internationally.

ENCYCLOPEDIAS AND DICTIONARIES

Black, John, Nigar Hashimzade, and Gareth Myles. *Dictionary of Economics.* 3rd ed. New York: Oxford University Press, 2009.
  Contains definitions of economics terms plus definitions related to investments, financial markets, and personal finance. Among the entries are the exchange rate mechanism, creeping inflation, the cost-of-living index, positive economics, and Reaganomics. Appendices contain institutional acronyms, Nobel Prize winners, and additional websites.

Darnell, Adrian C. *A Dictionary of Econometrics*. Brookfield, VT: Edward Elgar, 1994.

Designed primarily for faculty and students of graduate and postgraduate economics, with entries focusing on econometrics. Bibliographic references included with each entry. Among the entries are anticorrelation, forecasting, integration, matrix algebras, and random variables.

An Encyclopedia of Macroeconomics. Edited by Brian Snowdon and Howard R. Vane. Northampton, MA: Edward Elgar, 2003.

The stated goal of this encyclopedia is to provide a major reference book for undergraduates, postgraduates, and faculty in the field of macroeconomics. Contributors to entries are faculty from the United States, the United Kingdom, Amsterdam, and Canada, among other countries. Each entry provides detailed descriptions of macroeconomic terms (with cross-references) and a bibliography. Among the entries are income policy, the expectations-segmented Phillips curve, aggregated demand management, and nominal gross domestic product. Additional entries discuss major contributors to the field, such as Milton Friedman, Michal Kalecki, John Maynard Keynes, and Robert J. Barro.

Knopf, Kenyon. *A Lexicon of Economics*. San Diego, CA: Academic Press, 1991.

Provides definitions of economic terms and concepts ,including the budget line, deregulation, economic development, the gold standard, real wages, and the Robinson-Patman Act.

New Palgrave Dictionary of Economics Online (http://www.dictionaryof economics.com/dictionary).

Searchable (by topic and contributor) online version of the classic economics dictionary. Definitions are provided for terms and names of prominent economists. Entries are from both the first (1987) and second (2008) print editions. Each entry contains an abstract, key words, the article itself, cross-references, a bibliography, and information on creating citations. Cross-references are hot linked so that researchers can readily access related articles. Entries include approval voting, Nicholas Kaldor, John Maynard Keynes, tariffs, Ida Tarbell, and wage curve. New articles are added to the database. Libraries may also opt to purchase print editions:

The New Palgrave Dictionary of Economics. Edited by John Eatwell, Murray Millgate, and Peter Newman. New York: Stockton Press, 1987. 4 volumes.
The New Palgrave Dictionary of Economics. 2nd ed. Edited by Stephen A. Durlauf and Lawrence E. Blume. New York: Palgrave Macmillan, 2008. 8 volumes.

O'Connor, David E. *Encyclopedia of the Global Economy: A Guide for Students and Researchers*. Westport, CT: Greenwood Press, 2006. 2 volumes.

Volume 1 contains 168 entries related to key topics regarding the international economy. Illustrated with photographs and charts and close to 100 tables. Articles are cross-referenced and contain bibliographic citations. Topics covered include international trade, multilateral environmental agreements, terms of trade, the World Bank Group, cartel, and the Bretton Woods system. A glossary of selected terms is provided after the main A-to-Z encyclopedia entries in volume 1. Volume 2 consists of primary documents and statistical data. Sixty primary documents are organized under 10 headings: population, poverty reduction, economic growth and sustainable development, international trade, regional integration in the global trading system, foreign direct investment and corporate social responsibility, global labor markets and labor rights, the environment and sustainable development, consumer rights and sustainable consumption, and quality of life and economic justice.

The Oxford Encyclopedia of Economic History. Joel Mokyr, Editor-in-Chief. New York: Oxford University Press, 2003. 5 volumes.

Contains approximately 900 entries arranged alphabetically. Additionally, there are topic outlines of entries (e.g., the entries under "Regulation: include "Deregulation" and "Energy Regulation"). Entries include terms, names of countries, names of individuals (e.g., John Maynard Keynes), and names of industries. The entries are written in historical context. For instance, for "Banking," the article is broken down by time periods: classical antiquity, the Middle Ages and early modern period, and the modern period.

The Princeton Encyclopedia of the World Economy. Edited by Kenneth A. Reinert and Runkishen S. Rajan. Princeton, NJ: Princeton University Press, 2009. 2 volumes.

Selects entry topics within six major categories: concepts and principles, models and theory, institutions and agreements, politics and instruments, analysis and tools, and actions and special issues. Entries, arranged in alphabetical order, include health and globalization, the General Agreement of Tariff and Trade, the Global Environment Facility, fair trade, the dollar standard, the Latin American debt crisis, the World Bank, tariffs, and joint ventures. Entries are cross-referenced and contain bibliographical references.

Rosenberg, Jerry M. *The Concise Encyclopedia of the Great Recession 2007–2010.* Lanham, MD: Scarecrow Press, 2010.

Focuses on the economic recession with entries arranged alphabetically and cross-referenced. Entries cover terms, names of legislation, companies, and organizations. Among the entries are Lehman Brothers, the stimulus plan, subprime, Ben Bernanke, and the American Recovery and Reinvestment Act of 2009.

Rutherford, Donald. *Routledge Dictionary of Economics.* 2nd ed. London: Routledge, 2002.

Entries are listed alphabetically, defining terms with cross-references provided. Some of the entries include bibliographic references. The dictionary not only includes definitions of economics terms but also contains entries for individuals, names of key legislation, agencies, and organizations. Appendix A contains a list of currencies of the world, and Appendix B contains world stock market indices and subject classifications as used in the *Journal of Economic Literature* and *The Economic Journal*. The dictionary also includes a list of acronyms and abbreviations.

The Worldmark Encyclopedia of National Economies. Edited by Sara Pendergast and Tom Pendergast. Detroit: Gale Group, 2002. 4 volumes.
Provides "comprehensive overviews of the economic structure and current climate of 198 countries and territories" (preface). Each entry provides information about economic conditions and statistical data that allow comparisons to be made between countries. Each entry has the following components: country overview; overview of economy; politics, government, and taxation; infrastructure, power, and communications; economic sectors; agriculture; industry; services; international trade; money; poverty and wealth; working conditions; country history and economic development; future trends; dependencies; and bibliography. Entries include charts and tables with statistical data.

BIOGRAPHICAL SOURCES

A Biographical Dictionary of Dissenting Economists. 2nd ed. Edited by Philip Arestis and Malcolm Sawyer. Northampton, MA: Edward Elgar, 2000.
Focuses on dissenters in the field and examines how they came to adopt the views they did. Among those covered are John Kenneth Galbraith, Thorstein Veblen, John Maynard Keynes, Robert Heilbroner, and Nicholas Kaldor. Bibliographical references are included with each essay.

A Biographical Dictionary of Women Economists. Edited by Robert W. Dimand, Mary Ann Dimand, and Evelyn L. Forget. Northampton, MA: Edward Elgar, 2000.
Biographical profiles of women economists, their lives, and their contributions, with bibliography works by and about each individual. Among those profiled are Edith Abbott, Joan Robinson, Elizabeth Boody Schumpeter, and Rose Director Friedman.

Blaug, Mark. *Great Economists since Keynes.* 2nd ed. Northampton, MA: Edward Elgar, 1998.
Profiles 100 economists, their lives, and their contributions to economic thought. Each entry includes a photograph, an essay about the individual, and a list of both primary and secondary literature.

Breit, William, and Barry T. Hirsch. *Lives of the Laureates: Twenty-Three Nobel Economists.* 5th ed. Cambridge, MA: MIT Press, 2009.
Features autobiographical essays of Nobel laureates, including Paul Samuelson, Milton Friedman, James M. Buchanan, Franco Modigliani, Douglass C. North, Robert M. Solow, and George J. Stigler.

Cicarelli, James, and Julianne Cicarelli. *Distinguished Women Economists.* Westport, CT: Greenwood Press, 2003.
Fifty-one biographical profiles of notable women in the field of economics. Each entry provides an introduction, a biographical sketch, a summary of

contributions, and a bibliography. Among those profiled are Jane Haldimand Marcet (1769–1858), Edith Abbott (1876–1957), Alice M. Rivlin (1931–), and Diane C. Swonk (1962–).

Nobel Laureates in Economic Sciences: A Biographical Dictionary. Edited by Bernard S. Katz. New York: Garland Publishing, 1989.
  Detailed biographers of Nobel Prize winners in economics through 1988. Provides detailed entries of lives and major economic contributions of such notables as Paul Samuelson, Wassily Leontief, Frederick August von Hayak, Milton Friendman, George J. Stigler, and Robert Merton Solow.

Who's Who in Economics. 4th ed. Edited by Mark Blaug and Howard R. Vane. Northampton, MA: Edward Elgar, 2003.
  Profiles living economists whose articles published from 1990 to 2000 have been most frequently cited. Essays are written by those profiled and include biographical data, principal field of interest, publications, and career.

HANDBOOK

The Handbook of Economic Methodology. Edited by John B. Davis, D. Wade Hands, and Uskali Maki. Northampton, MA: Edward Elgar, 1998.
  Provides detailed essays in the field of economic methodology. Topics are listed alphabetically with essays and bibliographical references. Essays cover the methodology of scientific research programs, Granger causality, and positive-normative distinction. Major contributors to the field are covered, including James M. Buchanan, John R. Hicks, and Alfred Marshall, among others.

ECONOMICS STATISTICS SOURCES

A major component of economic research is locating statistics related to indicators and data, such as the Consumer Price Index, gross domestic product, and population data. Included in this section are sources for both the United States and international data. Major sources of U.S. data are from agencies, notably, the U.S. Department of Commerce, the U.S. Department of Labor, and the U.S. Department of Labor. Sources of international data include the World Bank, the International Monetary Fund, the United Nations, and the Organization for Economic Cooperation and Development.

Business Statistics of the United States: Patterns of Economic Change. Edited by Cornelia J. Strawser. Lanham, MD: Bernan Press, 2010.
  This source "is a basic desk reference for anyone requiring statistics on the U.S. economy" (preface). This source contains approximately 3,500

economic time series covering the time since World War II and, for 200 key series, the time period from 1929 to 1948. The data are obtained mostly from federal government sources. Included is an overview, "Business Statistics in the Great Recession." Part A, "The U.S. Economy," contains annual values for major economic indicators, including national income and product, industrial production and capacity utilization, income distribution and poverty, consumer income and spending, foreign trade and finance, and employment, hours, and earnings. Part B, "Industry Profiles," includes the structure of the North American Industry Classification System, product and income by industry, and key industry sectors. Part B, "Historical Statistics," contains selected historical economic data (e.g., gross domestic product and industrial production and capacity utilization). Part D is titled "Regional and State Data (Per Capita Personal Income, United States and Selected States)." Includes an index.

Econ Data & Links (http://zimmer.csufresno.edu/~johnsh/econ/econ _EDL.htm).
Links to U.S. and international economic data. Also contains links to resources related to economic information sources.

Economagic.com: Economic Time Series Page (http://www.economagic.com).
Collection of links to economic time-series data (in table and chart formats). Contains data for U.S. population, gross domestic product, Consumer Price Index, employment and unemployment, Producer Price Index, data by U.S. state, and international statistics, including those from the Central Bank of Europe and the Bank of Japan and the Economic Planning Agency of Japan. Also features links to related sites of interest.

Economic Indicators.gov (U.S. Department of Commerce, Economics and Statistics Administration) (http://www.economicindicators.gov).
Links to statistical data for gross domestic product, new residential sales, new residential construction, personal income and outlays, U.S. international transactions, advance monthly sales for retail and food services, advance report on durable goods, and construction put in place.

Economic Report of the President (http://www.gpoaccess.gov/eop).
Contains the Economic Report of the President and the Annual Report of the Council for Economic Advisers. Focuses on the economic year in review and projections for the future; topics include labor force, health care, productivity, energy, and climate change. Report contains bibliographical references. The Annual Report of the Council for Economic Advisers contains a narrative review with statistical tables related to income, employment, and production. Among statistics found are those related to gross domestic product, population by age-group, and foreign exchange rates.

Economic Research (Federal Reserve Bank of St. Louis) (http://research .stlouisfed.org/fred2).

FRED (Federal Reserve Economic Data) is a database of U.S. economic time series pertaining to interest rates, gross domestic product and components, U.S. financial data, regional data, Producer Price Indexes, exchange rates, employment and population, Consumer Price Indexes, business/fiscal, banking, and U.S. trade and international transactions.

FedStats (http://www.fedstats.gov).
Searchable database provides statistics from approximately 100 federal government agencies. Search by topic, state, geography from U.S. agencies, published collections of statistics, agency websites, agency websites by subject, selected agency and online databases, and databases within agency websites.

International Monetary Fund (http://www.imf.org/external/index.htm).
The International Monetary Fund (IMF) "is an organization of 187 countries, working to foster global monetary cooperation, secure financial stability, facilitate international trade, promote high employment and sustainable economic growth, and reduce poverty around the world" (website). The IMF publishes a range of time-series data on IMF lending, exchange rates, and other economic and financial indicators. Key publications include *International Financial Statistics* and *Balance of Payments Statistics*. *International Financial Statistics* contains data for 200 countries, including exchange rates, fund accounts, and main global and country economic indicators. *Balance of Payments Statistics* provides annual aggregate and detailed time series for balance of payments and international investment position for countries and provides world and regional tables of balance of payments, components, and aggregates.

LexisNexis Statistical Insight (http://library.lexisnexis.com/ws_display.asp ?filter=Statistical%20Overview).
Database contains data from federal agencies, commercial publishers, associations, international intergovernmental organizations, research organizations, and state agencies. Provides capability of searching between 200,000 and 500,000 tables with advanced search tables. Also provides an abstracts search to find summaries of statistical publications Contains coverage of the *American Statistics Index (ASI)*, the *Statistical Reference Index (SRI)*, and *Index to International Statistics (IIS)*. *The American Statistics Index* abstracts and indexes federal statistical publications. The Statistical Reference Index abstracts and indexes publications of state and private-sector sources, among which are professional and trade associations, business organizations, commercial publishers, universities, state governments, and independent research organizations.. *The Index to International Statistics* abstracts and indexes statistical titles from international intergovernmental organizations, among which are the Organization for Economic Cooperation and Development, the United Nations, and the World Bank. LexisNexis also distributes hardbound volumes of *SRI, ASI,* and *IIS*. Included is a microfiche library of the full text of most titles indexed.

Monthly Labor Review, U.S. Department of Labor, Bureau of Labor Statistics (BLS), (http://www.bls.gov/opub/mlr).

Access to full text is available on the BLS website. Current and archival issues (back to 1981) are included. Each issue contains labor month in review, precis (focusing on a specific topic, e.g., women and higher education), book reviews, and current labor statistics, featuring 55 tables of current labor statistics. Data are arranged within the following categories: employment and unemployment tables, employment projections tables, prices and living conditions tables, compensation and working conditions tables, compensation and working conditions tables, productivity tables, and foreign labor statistics tables.

Organisation for Economic Cooperation and Development (OECD) (http://www.oecd.org).

"OECD brings together the governments of countries committed to democracy and the market economy from around the world to: support sustainable economic growth, boost employment, raise living standards, maintain financial stability, assist other countries' economic development, and contribute to growth in world trade" (website). Major resources published by the OECD include the *OECD Factbook, Economic Outlook* (available online), and *Country Studies* (print and online). *The OECD Factbook* (print and online) contains statistical charts and analysis for each country covered: population growth, gross domestic product per capita, net migration rate, production and income, and so on. Additionally, statistics are available via OECD data warehouse and databases and key tables, and statistics are provided for economic projections, monthly economic indicators, productivity and prices, and purchasing power, among other data.

Statistical Abstract of the United States (U.S. Census Bureau) (http://www .census.gov/compendia/statab).

"The *Statistical Abstracts*, published since 1878, is the authoritative and comprehensive summary of statistics on the social, political, and economic organization of the United States" (website). Provides both current and historical editions from 1878 on in full text. Categories of statistics include income, expenditures, poverty, and wealth; population; prices; manufactures; social insurance and human services; wholesale and retail trade; foreign commerce and aid; energy and utilities; agriculture; energy and utilities; and education.

Statistical Yearbook. Annuaire Statiistique, by the United Nations, Statistical Office. New York: United Nations. Annual.

Annual compilation of international economic, social, and environmental statistics on over 200 countries and areas. Covers statistics for balance of payments, labor force, industrial production, national accounts, wages and prices, and so on. Provides charts and tables, technical notes, definitions, and classifications.

Survey of Current Business, U.S. Department of Labor, Bureau of Labor Statistics (http://www.bea.gov/scb).

Articles contain current national, international, regional, and industry estimates; describe the methodologies used to prepare the estimates; provide
information about major revisions; and discuss ongoing innovations and
generally current awareness of the issues and initiatives of the Bureau of
Economic Analysis. Provides charts and tales of economic estimates.
Allows searching of the survey, selecting specific time periods of issues
(e.g., 1934–1949). Data presented include gross domestic product,
regional statistics, exports and imports, corporate profits, and personal
consumption expenditures. Tables and charts are accompanied by narrative analysis of statistics and projections.

United Nations Economic Commission for Europe (http://www.unece.org/).
Searchable database allows the creation of tables for statistics related to
national accounts, price indices, the labor force, external economic relations, industrial production, and country overviews.

U.S. Census Bureau (http://www.census.gov).
According to its mission statement, the U.S. Census Bureau "serves as the
leading source of quality data about the nation's people and economy.
We honor privacy, protect confidentiality, share our expertise globally,
and conduct our work openly. We are guided on this mission by
our strong and capable workforce, our readiness to innovate, and our
abiding commitment to our customers" (website). Collects data regarding population and housing (every 10 years), economic census (every
five years), census of governments (every five years), the American
Community Survey (annually), economic indicators (various release
schedules), and surveys analyzing social, economic and geographic
data. Provides population and housing censuses in full text (PDF)
from 1790 to 2000. Provides economic censuses for 2002 and 1997 in full
text (PDF).

U.S. Department of Commerce, Bureau of Economic Analysis (BEA) (http://
www.bea.gov).
Source of economic data: national (gross domestic product [GDP], consumer spending, personal income and outlays, corporate profits, and
fixed assets), regional (GDP by state and metropolitan areas, state and
local areas, and personal income), international (balance of payments,
trade in goods and services, international services, and operations of
multinational companies), and industry (annual industry accounts). The
BEA website also features interactive data tables, papers and working
papers, a digital library, a newsroom, conferences and meetings, and
links to its publication *Survey of Current Business*.

U.S. Department of Commerce, International Trade Administration (http://
www.trade.gov).
Provides annual and quarterly trade data via the searchable database
TradeStats Express. Also contains U.S. Export Fact Sheet containing an
export overview with current data and a "trade spotlight" focusing on
specific trade markets.

U.S. Department of Labor, Bureau of Labor Statistics (http://www.bls.gov).
    Contains economic news releases and databases, tables, and calculators by
    subject. Statistics are organized within major categories: inflation and
    prices, employment, unemployment, pay and benefits, spending and
    time use, productivity, workplace injuries, international data, employ-
    ment projections, regional resources, and historical news release tables.
    Tools are available to create customized statistical data. Tutorials are
    available regarding accessing data.

United States Economy at a Glance, Bureau of Labor Statistics (http://
    www.bls.gov/eag/eag.us.htm).
    Contains U.S. economy monthly data: Consumer Price Index, Producer
    Price Index, unemployment rate, U.S. Import Price Index, and average
    hourly earnings and quarterly data on employment cost index and
    productivity.

World Bank (http://www.worldbank.org).
    The mission of the World Bank is to "fight poverty with passion and profes-
    sionalism for lasting results and to help people help themselves and their
    environment by providing resources, sharing knowledge, building capac-
    ity and forging partnerships in the public and private sectors" (website).
    Contains an online data source, World Development Indicators (http://
    data.worldbank.org/data-catalog/world-development-indicators), a col-
    lection of development indicators including national, regional, and global
    estimates. Also, databases are available for individual country searches to
    locate data on gross domestic product, population, life expectancy, infra-
    structure, health, and economic policy and external debt.

PERIODICAL INDEXES AND FULL-TEXT DATABASES

Economic literature from journals may be found in *Business Source
Premier, ABI/INFORM, ScienceDirect,* and *JSTOR* Additionally, there are
specialized indexes and abstracts and databases with some providing
full-text coverage of articles and other publications.

Abstracts of Working Papers in Economics (http://journals.cambridge.org/
    action/displayJournal?jid=PYE).
    Provides full bibliographic information, including working paper series
    addresses, Web links, price and availability, and JEL classification codes
    and complete abstracts. Each issue includes approximately 550 papers,
    indexed by author and issuing institution, Contains a key word index
    and permuted title index.

EconLit (http://www.aeaweb.org/econlit/index.php).
    Published by the American Economics Association, provides international
    coverage of economic literature indexes and abstracts, including journal
    articles, books, book reviews, collected volumes online, working papers,

and dissertations. Available through the American Economics Association and through the vendors CSA and Dialog.

National Bureau of Economic Research (NBER) (http://www.nber.org).
The NBER "is a private, nonprofit, nonpartisan research organization dedicated to promoting a greater understanding of how the economy works" (website). The site contains a repository of working papers on various topics related to the economy by experts in the field. Includes a catalog of books of interest for purchase and full-text access to their periodical publication *NBER Reporter Online*.

MAJOR ECONOMICS JOURNALS

Applied Economics (http://www.tandf.co.uk/journals/titles/00036846.asp)
Decisions in Economics and Finance (http://www.springerlink.com/content/100169)
Economic Affairs (http://www.blackwellpublishing.com/journal.asp?ref=0265-0665)
Economic History Review (http://www.blackwellpublishing.com/journal.asp?ref=0013-0117)
The Economic Journal (http://www.blackwellpublishing.com/journal.asp?ref=0013-0133)
Economic Theory (http://www.springerlink.com/content/100511)
The Economist (http://www.economist.com)
Economy and Society (http://www.tandf.co.uk/journals/routledge/03085147.html)
Explorations in Economic History (http://www.sciencedirect.com/science/journal/00144983)
Global Economic Review (http://www.tandf.co.uk/journals/titles/1226508x.asp)
International Journal of Social Economics (http://www.emeraldinsight.com/products/journals/journals.htm?id=ijse)
Journal of Economic and Social Measurement (http://www.iospress.nl/loadtop/load.php?isbn=07479662)
Journal of Economic Literature (http://www.aeaweb.org/jel/index.php)
Journal of the History of Economic Thought (http://journals.cambridge.org/action/displayJournal?jid=HET)
Quarterly Journal of Economics (http://www.mitpressjournals.org/loi/qjec)
Review of Economics and Statistics (http://www.mitpressjournals.org/loi/rest)
Review of Law and Economics (http://www.bepress.com/rle)
Review of World Economics (http://www.springerlink.com/content/112760)

MAJOR WEBSITES

American Economic Association (AEA) (http://www.vanderbilt.edu/AEA).
The purposes of the AEA are "the encouragement of economic research, especially the historical and statistical study of the actual conditions of

industrial life; the issue of publications on economic subjects; and the encouragement of perfect freedom of economic discussion" (website). The AEA is the publisher of EconLit and also has a link to Resources for Economists on the Internet (http://rfe.org).

American Institute for Economic Research (http://www.aier.org).
   "Conducts independent, scientific, economic research to educate individuals, thereby advancing their personal interests and those of the Nation" (website). Focuses on the consumer, presenting news reports, advice, and publications for purchase.

Association for Social Economics (http://www.socialeconomics.org).
   The association "was formed to advance scholarly research and writing about the great questions of economics, human dignity, ethics, and philosophy" (website). Contains news on conferences, a book review list, and a forum for open discussions.

International Economics Network (http://www.internationalecono mics.net).
   Contains links to resources related to international business and economics.

Yahoo! Directory Economics (http://dir.yahoo.com/Social_Science/ Economics).
   Contains links to resources related to, among other topics, economists, behavioral economics, recession, journals, libraries, and the global economy.

Yahoo! News U.S. Economy (http://news.yahoo.com/business/us-economy).
   Current news reports on the U.S. economy, economic indicators, and stock quotes.

9

Money and Banking

Money is as a medium of payment for goods and services or a measure of value. Throughout world history, various commodities have been used as money: gold, silver, seashells, and beads. Beginning in the seventeenth century, the most common forms of money were coins and paper notes—metals for coins have been used for several thousand years.

Early forms of banking date back to Mesopotamia, where temples, royal palaces, and private homes served as repositories for commodities. In Babylon, records of loans kept by the temples have been discovered. The industry evolved, and in medieval Europe, organizations developed with the charge of depositing and tending money. Beginning in the sixteenth century, European banks developed and were divided into two types: exchange banks and banks of deposit. Over the next few centuries, major banks to develop in Europe included the Bank of Venice, the Bank of England, the Bank of Germany, and the Bank of France.

The First Bank of the United States was created in 1791 and the Second Bank of the United States in 1816. In the late nineteenth century, the United States had an unregulated and decentralized system that caused a series of financial panics. The 1913 Federal Reserve Act created the Federal Reserve, which included a board of governors and 12 regional banks.

This chapter focuses on information sources related to U.S. and international banks: encyclopedias, dictionaries, handbooks, journals, and trade association websites.

ENCYCLOPEDIAS AND DICTIONARIES

Allen, Larry. *The Encyclopedia of Money.* 2nd ed. Santa Barbara, CA: ABC-CLIO, 2009.
  Encyclopedia about money and related issues, including banking, inflation, and financial crises. Entries are in alphabetical order with cross-
  references, an extensive bibliography, and bibliographic references at
  the end of each article. Illustrations are included. Among the entries are
  Goldsmith Bankers, First Bank of the United States, Federal Reserve
  System, pound sterling, banking crises, and Bank of England.

Clark, John. *International Dictionary of Banking and Finance.* Chicago: Glenlake
  Publishing Company and Fitzroy Dearborn Publishers, 1999.
  Provides definitions of specialist terms in banking and general finance for
  students and professionals. Cross-referenced entries. Terms defined
  include blue-sky, blocked currency, European Monetary Institute, bank
  reconciliation statement, and bank statement.

A Dictionary of Finance and Banking. 3rd ed. New York: Oxford University
  Press, 2005.
  Designed for professionals, students, and private investors. Contains 5,000
  entries of terms related to banking, foreign exchanges, money markets,
  business loans and debt collecting, and so on. Entries include bank holi-
  days, bank rate, audit, Glass-Steagall Act of 1933, and home banking. Provides cross-references.

Fitch, Thomas P. *Dictionary of Banking Terms.* 5th ed. Hauppauge, NY: Barron's
  Educational Series, 2006.
  Contains definitions for over 3,000 terms related to banking, electronic
  commerce, money management, finance, and legal regulations. Cross-
  references plus an abbreviations and acronyms section and a list of world
  currencies by country. Among the terms defined are collateral loan, bank
  reserves, Fannie Mae, Fair Credit Reporting Act, Federal Deposit Insurance Corporation, receiving bank, and Federal Reserve Board.

Markham, Jerry W. *A Financial History of the United States.* Armonk, NY: M. E.
  Sharpe, 2002. 3 volumes.
  Comprised of three volumes: volume 1: *From Christopher Columbus to the
  Robber Barons, 1492–1900*; volume 2: *From J. P. Morgan to the Individual
  Investor (1900–1970)*; and volume 3: *From the Age of Derivatives to the New
  Millennium (1970–2001)*. Detailed essays on specific time periods covering
  the history of banks, the development of corporations, investments,
  panics, profiles of key individuals, and monetary issues. Bibliographical
  references are provided.

The New Palgrave Dictionary of Money and Finance. Edited by Peter Newman,
  Murray Milgate, and John Eatwell. London: Macmillan Press; New York:
  Stockton Press, 1992. 3 volumes.
  Provides 1,008 entries, arranged in alphabetical sequence and cross-
  referenced and with a list of acronyms. Among the entries are Federal

Deposit Insurance Corporation, overdrafts, Islamic banking, mutual savings institutions, Bank for International Settlements, Bank of England, Glass-Steagall Act, banking crises, and Banking Act of 1935. Also contains topics related to investments, accounting, and financial markets.

Woelfel, Charles J. *The Dictionary of Banking: Over 5,000 Terms Defined and Explained. A Bankline Publication.* Chicago: Probus Publishing, 1994.
Definitions of terms related to banking plus an acronym glossary. Among the entries are annual percentage rate, Federal Home Mortgage Corporation, Federal Reserve Board of Governors, and new money.

ALMANACS AND HANDBOOKS

Handbook of International Banking. Edited by Andrew Mullneux and Victor Murinde. Northampton, MA: Edward Elgar, 2005.
Comprised of a series of essays by experts in the field, including professors and research analysts, related to various aspects of international banking. Essays are grouped within four parts: part I: The Globalization of Banking; part II: Banking Structures and Functions; part III: Banking Risks, Crises, and Regulations; and part IV: The Evolving International Financial Architecture. Topics covered by essays include the International Monetary Fund, U.S. banking regulation, free banking, and international banking crises. Bibliographical references and statistical figures, tables, and exhibits are provided.

Plunkett's Banking, Mortgages, & Credit Industry Almanac. Edited by Jack W. Plunkett. Houston: Plunkett Research. Annual.
Divided into two main sections: Banking Industry and Banking and Lending 350. Section 1 includes a glossary of terms, industry statistics, trends, and directories of trade associations and websites. Section 2 contains one-page profiles for each of the Banking and Lending 350—these companies profiled are within the industry sectors of banking mortgage and credit. Each company entry includes name, address, telephone, fax, key executives, number of employees, sales and profit statistics, divisions and affiliate listings, compensation for executives, and growth plans.

DIRECTORIES

Search for banks on *Standard & Poor's NetAdvantage*, Dun & Bradstreet, *Hoover's*, and *Mergent Online* (for full descriptions, see Chapter 3).

The Bank Directory. Skokie, IL: Accuity (Formerly Thomson Financial Publishing). Published in June and December. 5 volumes.
Also known as the Banker's Blue Book, a comprehensive directory of banks around the world. Comprised of five volumes: volume 1: *United States, A–L*; volume 2: *United States M–W and U.S. Dependencies*; volume 3:

World A–I; volume 4: *World J–Z*; and volume 5: *Worldwide Correspondents and Resource Guide* (suppliers to the marketplace). Contains data including names, addresses, telephone numbers, association memberships, national routing codes, branch offices, industry statistics and rankings, standard settlement instructions, credit ratings, and a resource guide featuring suppliers to the marketplace.

Mergent/Moody's Bank and Finance Manual (http://www.mergent.com).
Digitized back issues of Moody's Manuals from 1928 to the present in digitized format. Entries include name, address, telephone subsidiaries, officers, income statements, balance sheets, ticker symbol, number of employees, and number of shareholders.

Yahoo! Directory: Banks (http://dir.yahoo.com/Business_and_Economy/ Shopping_and_Services/Financial_Services/Banking/Banks/?skw=yahoo +banks).
Search for banks by country and within categories: central banks, credit unions, development banks, and directories.

MAJOR GOVERNMENT AGENCIES, ORGANIZATIONS, AND STATISTICS SOURCES

Asian Development Bank (ADB) (http://www.adb.org).
The "ADB is an international development finance institution whose mission is to help its developing member countries reduce poverty and improve the quality of life of their people" (website). Publishes key indicators for Asia and the Pacific in digital and print formats, featuring tables and charts with data on national accounts, prices, government finance, trade, balance of payments, money and banking, external debt, population, labor force, and social indicators.

Bank for International Settlements (http://www.bis.org).
"The Bank for International Settlements (BIS) is an international organisation which fosters international monetary and financial cooperation and serves as a bank for central banks. The BIS fulfils this mandate by acting as: a forum to promote discussion and policy analysis among central banks and within the international financial community; a centre for economic and monetary research; a prime counterparty for central banks in their financial transactions; agent or trustee in connection with international financial operations" (website). International financial statistics compiled by the BIS include cross-border lending and borrowing of internationally active banks in key financial centres, including offshore centers; issuing activity in international and domestic securities markets; operations in over-the-counter and exchange-traded derivative markets; and effective exchange rate indices for 58 economies.

BANKSCOPE (https://bankscope2.bvdep.com/version-20101026/Home .serv?product=scope2006).

Provides financial information for over 28,000 banks worldwide. Contains data for European banks, North American banks, Japanese commercial banks, and sogo banks and over 4,100 major banks. Detailed financials include balance sheet and ratios and ratings from Fitch, Moody's and Standard & Poor's.

European Banking Federation (FBE) (http://www.fbe.be).
The FBE is the united voice of the banks in the European Union and the European Free Trade Association countries.

European Central Bank (ECB) (http://www.ecb.int).
The ECB and the national European central banks together constitute the Eurosystem, the central banking system for the Euro area. Contains the Statistical Data Warehouse, containing selected indicators for the Euro area: U.S. dollar/euro exchange rate; money, banking, and financial markets; banknotes and coins; and Euro area accounts.

Federal Deposit Insurance Corporation (FDIC) (http://www.fdic.gov).
The mission of the FDIC is as follows: "The Federal Deposit Insurance Corporation (FDIC) is an independent agency created by the Congress to maintain stability and public confidence in the nation's financial system by:

- insuring deposits,
- examining and supervising financial institutions for safety and soundness and consumer protection, and
- managing receiverships" (website)

The FDIC publishes the online *Statistics on Banking* to locate quarterly and historical statistics. *Statistics at a Glance* provides the latest quarterly and historical data for FDIC-insured institutions, the FDIC insurance fund, and the number of FDIC employees beginning with the June 2001 issue. Statistics provided in FDIC publications include numbers of new charters, commercial banks, savings institutions, and problem institutions. The *Quarterly Banking Profile* is a quarterly publication that provides the earliest comprehensive summary of financial results for all FDIC-insured institutions. The *FDIC Quarterly* provides a comprehensive summary of the most current financial results for the banking industry, plus feature articles, including those that analyze economic and banking trends at national and regional levels that may affect risk exposure of FDIC-insured institutions and those that discuss issues affecting the banking system and the development of regulatory policy. Information and statistics are also available via searchable databases, including the FDIC Institution Directory, which enables searching institutions insured by the FDIC, including holding companies, bank or thrift, and specific offices. Other information and statistics available include regional economic conditions (economic information at state, metropolitan statistical area, and county levels), summary of deposits, statistics on depository institutions, reports of changes to FDIC financial institutions and office structure, and the Central Data Repository. Other resources of the FDIC include consumer protection advice and materials, regulations and examinations, and news and events.

Federal Reserve System, Board of Governors (http://www.federalreserve.gov).
Commonly known as the "Fed," the Central Bank of the United States, founded by Congress in 1913 "to provide the nation with a safer, more flexible and stable monetary and financial system." The duties of the Federal Reserve are "conducting the nation's monetary policy by influencing the monetary and credit conditions in the economy in pursuit of maximum employment, stable prices, and moderate long-term interest rates; supervising and regulating banking institutions to ensure the safety and soundness of the nation's banking and financial system and to protect the credit rights of consumers; maintaining the stability of the financial system and containing systemic risk that may arise in financial markets, and providing financial services to depository institutions, the U.S. government, and foreign official institutions, including playing a major role in operating the nation's payments system." (website). For further information about the Fed, a guide is accessible online, The Federal Reserve: Purposes and Functions (http://www.federalreserve.gov/pf/pf.htm), providing an overview and discussion of monetary policy and the economy, the implementation of monetary policy, the Federal Reserve in the international sphere, supervision and regulation, consumer and community affairs, and the Federal Reserve in the U.S. Payment System.

A source of research data on banks and banking is the following:
Federal Reserve Bulletin (http://www.federalreserve.gov/pubs/bulletin/default.htm).

Began publication in 1914 to present policy issues by the Fed. Contains legal developments and topic research section by authors from the Fed Board's research and statistics, monetary affairs, international finance, banking supervision and regulation, consumer and community affairs, Reserve bank operations, and legal divisions. Online access is free, and an email notification is included to alert subscribers about new articles. A print-based compilation of articles and legal developments is published annually. Prior to 2009, the bulletin contained a *Statistical Supplement to the Federal Reserve Bulletin*.

Data Sources Web page (http://www.federalreserve.gov/pubs/supplement/statsupdata/statsupdata.htm).
After 2009, data are located on this site rather than in the Statistical Supplement. Source of data for money stock and bank credit; policy instruments (e.g., Federal Reserve Bank interest rates); Federal Reserve banks (e.g., Condition and Federal Reserve Note Statements); monetary and credit aggregates; commercial banking institutions, assets, and liabilities; financial markets; federal finance; securities markets and corporate finance; real estate (e.g., mortgage markets and new homes); consumer credit; flow of funds; interest and foreign exchange rates; U.S. branches and assets of foreign banks; small loans to business and farms; terms of

lending of commercial banks; U.S. international transactions, summary; and marketable U.S. Treasury bonds and notes.

Top 50 Bank Holding Companies http://www.ffiec.gov/nicpubweb/nicweb/Top50Form.aspx. Ranked by total assets.

The Federal Reserve is comprised of 12 districts. The following map from the Federal Reserve website illustrates the locations of each district.

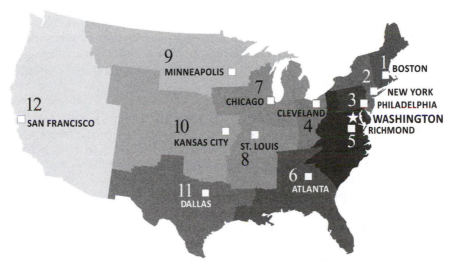

Source: http://www.federalreserve.gov/otherfrb.htm.

The Federal Reserve districts promote growth and financial stability and contributes to region and nation through regulatory oversight, financial services, and commitment to leadership and innovation:
Federal Reserve Bank of Boston (http://www.bos.frb.org)

Federal Reserve Bank of New York (http://www.newyorkfed.org/index.html)
Federal Reserve Bank of Philadelphia (http://www.philadelphiafed.org/index.cfm)
Federal Reserve Bank of Cleveland (http://www.clevelandfed.org)
Federal Reserve Bank of Richmond (http://www.richmondfed.org)
Federal Reserve Bank of Atlanta (http://www.frbatlanta.org)
Federal Reserve Bank of Chicago (http://www.chicagofed.org/webpages/index.cfm)
Federal Reserve Bank of St. Louis (http://www.stlouisfed.org)
Federal Reserve Bank of Minneapolis (http://www.minneapolisfed.org)
Federal Reserve Bank of Kansas City (http://www.kansascityfed.org)
Federal Reserve Bank of Dallas (http://www.dallasfed.org)
Federal Reserve Bank of San Francisco (http://www.frbsf.org)
Foreign Central Bank Websites (http://www.bis.org/cbanks.htm).
Prepared by the Bank for International Settlements, contains links to central banks' websites.

International Monetary Fund (http://www.imf.org/external/index.htm).
    Contains money and banking-related data, among which are currency
    composition of official foreign exchange reserves, international financial
    statistics, representative rates for selective currencies, monetary and
    financial statistics, and exchange rate data. Also contains working papers
    in full text, annual reports, and periodical publications, including the
    IMF Economics Review.

Latin American Federation of Banks (FELABAN) (http://www.felaban.com).
    A nonprofit organization constituted in 1965 with its objectives to promote
    and facilitate contacts, understanding, and relationships among credit
    institutions in Latin America and to contribute to the economic develop-
    ment of Latin American countries and the reduction of poverty. Publishes
    a digital bulletin.

Mergent Online (http://www.mergent.com).
    Features industry reports for Europe, Asia Pacific, North America, and
    Latin America. Includes current and retrospective reports for banking
    (back to 2007). For each country in the "Geographic" section, data include
    an industry overview (current developments, industry size, and value
    [assets]), leading banks and summaries of their performance, and market
    outlook and key references (list of websites for major banking and finance
    organizations for each country).

SNL Financial (http://www.snl.com)
    Research firm that prepares corporate, financial (including banking) merg-
    ers and acquisitions, and news and analytics. Subscription-based service
    prepares branch analytics, detailed marketing demographics, branch
    mapping, and peer analytics.

Standard & Poor's NetAdvantage (http://www.netadvantage.standardand
    poors.com/NASApp/NetAdvantage/servlet/login?url=/NASApp/
    NetAdvantage/index.do).
    Select the Industry Surveys to locate reports that include banking. For
    banking, current and historical reports (12 years of statistics) are pro-
    vided in PDF and HTML formats. Contents of the Banking Industry Sur-
    veys cover current environment (study of trends, economic impact,
    regulations, net income, number of loans, and so on), industry profile
    (25 largest banking companies, trends, regulatory news, key industry
    ratios, and statistics), and industry references (a list of websites for peri-
    odicals, regulatory and federal agencies, market research firms, and trade
    associations).

U.S. Department of the Treasury (http://www.ustreas.gov).
    The basic functions of the Department of the Treasury include "managing
    Federal finances; Collecting taxes, duties and monies paid to and due to
    the U.S. and paying all bills of the U.S.; Currency and coinage; Managing
    Government accounts and the public debt; Supervising national banks
    and thrift institutions; Advising on domestic and international financial,
    monetary, economic, trade and tax policy; Enforcing Federal finance and

tax laws; Investigating and prosecuting tax evaders, counterfeiters, and forgers" (website). Features news releases about new currency and coins (including new designs), money facts and history, how to detect counterfeit money, a virtual tour about how coins are made, interest rate statistics, and reports about key legislation (e.g., the American Recovery and Investment Act).

U.S. Department of the Treasury. Internal Revenue Service (http://www.irs.gov/) (see also Chapter 14 for more information about the IRS). Publishes the *Treasury Bulletin*, which includes a combination of narrative, tables, and charts related to: Treasury issues, Federal fiscal operations, international financial statistics, profile of the economy, and Federal debt.

U.S. Mint (http://www.usmint.gov).
Created by Congress in 1792, the U.S. Mint's mission is as follows: "The primary mission of the United States Mint is to produce an adequate volume of circulating coinage for the nation to conduct its trade and commerce. In recent history circulating coin production has varied between 11 billion and 20 billion coins annually. In addition to producing coins, the United States Mint has other responsibilities, including the following: Distributing U.S. coins to the Federal Reserve banks and branches. Maintaining physical custody and protection of the Nation's $100 billion of U.S. gold and silver assets. Producing proof, uncirculated, and commemorative coins, and medals for sale to the general public. Manufacturing and selling platinum, gold, and silver bullion coins. Overseeing of production facilities in Denver, Philadelphia, San Francisco and West Point, as well as the U.S. Bullion Depository at Fort Knox, Kentucky" (website). Features current and back issues of annual reports, coin production figures, and information about U.S. Mint facilities and how coins are made.

Wharton Research Data Service (http://wrds.wharton.upenn.edu).
A Web-based business data research service from the Wharton School at the University of Pennsylvania, a research tool for academics. Contains the following databases related to banking:

Bank Regulatory—Accounting data for bank holding companies, commercial banks, savings banks, and savings-and-loan institutions.
FDIC—Federal Deposit Insurance Corporation database provides financial data and history of all entities filing the Report of Condition and Income (Call Report) and some savings institutions filing the OTS Thrift Financial Report.
Federal Reserve Bank Reports—Comprised of data collected from Federal Reserve banks. Contains foreign exchange, interest rates, and coincident state indexes (from the Federal Reserve Bank of Philadelphia).

World Bank (http://www.worldbank.org).
Largest provider of development assistance to low- and middle-income countries. Publishes statistics sources, including the World Development Indicators, Global Development Finance, World Bank Research Working Papers, and Quarterly External Debt Statistics.

PERIODICAL INDEXES AND FULL-TEXT DATABASES

In addition to locating information through *ABI/INFORM*, *Business Source Premier*, the *Wall Street Journal*, *JSTOR*, and *ScienceDirect*, the following specialized database is available:

ProQuest Banking Information Source (http://www.proquest.com/en-US/
catalogs/databases/detail/pq_banking_info.shtml).
Covers over 620 journals and provides full-text access to industry and professional newsletters, Stonier theses, and School of Bank marketing papers. Also accessible through Dialog.

PERIODICALS

ABA Banking Journal (http://www.ababj.com)
American Banker (http://www.americanbanker.com)
The Banker (http://www.thebanker.com)
Journal of Banking and Finance (http://www.elsevier.com/wps/find/journal
description.cws_home/505558/description#description)
Journal of Banking Regulation (http://www.palgrave-journals.com/jbr/index
.html)
Journal of Economics, Banking, and Finance (http://www.scientificjournals.org/
journals2008/j_of_economics1_2008.htm)
Journal of Money, Credit, and Banking (http://www.wiley.com/bw/journal.asp
?ref=0022-2879)
Journal of Money, Investment, and Banking (http://www.eurojournals.com/
JMIB.htm)
Mortgage Banking (http://mortgagebankingmagazine.com/default.htm)
Private Banker International (http://www.vrl-financial-news.com/wealth
-management/private-banker-intl.aspx)
The Review of Financial Studies (http://rfs.oxfordjournals.org)

TRADE ASSOCIATION WEBSITES

American Bankers Association (http://www.aba.com/default.htm).
"Represents banks of all sizes and charters and is the voice for the nation's $13 trillion banking industry and its 2 million employees" (website). Publisher of periodicals: *ABA Bank Compliance*, *ABA Bank Directors Briefing*, *ABA Bank Marketing*, *ABA Banking Journal*, *ABA Trust Letter*, *Community Banker*, *Consumer Credit Delinquency Bulletin*, and *Washington Perspective*.

American Bankruptcy Institute (http://www.abiworld.org).
Provides Congress and the public with analysis of bankruptcy issues. Contains Consumer Bankruptcy Center (advice to consumers) and news headlines and publishes *ABI Journal* and *ABI Law Review*.

Mortgage Bankers Association (http://www.mortgagebankers.org).
National association representing the real estate finance industry. Publishes forecasts and benchmarking studies.

CALCULATORS

BanxQuote (http://www.banx.com).
Locate mortgage, CD, and money market rates.

Bankrate.com (http://www.bankrate.com).
Contains calculators of mortgage payments, car loans, credit card payoff, savings, and debt management. Also contains news reports, mortgage rate trend index, and CD and money market rates.

Universal Currency Converter (http://www.xe.com/ucc).
Calculator of currency exchange rates.

10

Insurance

Insurance is defined, according to the Insurance Information Institute, as "a system to make large financial losses more affordable by pooling the risks of many individuals and business entities and transferring them to an insurance company or other large group in return for a premium" (*Glossary of Insurance and Risk Management Terms*). The earliest form of insurance was marine insurance, which dates back to Babylonia; life and health insurance has been chronicled as existing in ancient Greece and Rome. In colonial America, the earliest insurance companies included the Friendly Society of Charleston, South Carolina, in 1735, and the Corporation for the Relief of Poor and Distressed Presbyterian Ministers and for the Poor and Distressed Widows and Children of Presbyterian Ministers in 1759. In the nineteenth century, insurance companies were founded, including Travelers Insurance Company in 1863 (Travelers is credited with the first accident insurance) and Prudential Insurance Company in 1875. The twentieth century marked the time of the beginning of Blue Cross and Blue Shield group hospitalization and medical insurance and the Social Security Act, passed by Congress in 1935. In the current century, the Health Care Reform Act was passed by Congress in 2010.

Major types of insurance are life/health and property/casualty. Property insurance provides coverage in the event of loss or damage to property, including homes, automobiles, and luxury items, and casualty covers liability of an individual or organization that results from negligence that causes injury and property damage. Life insurance is a policy that provides a guaranteed payment to a designated beneficiary on the death of the insured individual. Health insurance covers medical expenses for hospital stays, doctor appointments, and specific treatments. Health insurance can be purchased by individuals or provided through an employer.

DICTIONARIES

Glossary of Insurance and Risk Management Terms. 11th ed. Dallas: International Risk Management Institute, Inc., 2007.
   Features definitions and cross-references. Includes a listing of state regulatory agencies.

Rubin, Harvey W. *Dictionary of Insurance Terms.* 5th ed. Hauppauge, NY: Barron's Educational Series, 2008.
   Contains concise definitions of insurance-related terms, with cross-references and a separate list of abbreviations and acronyms.

GUIDES

Baldwin, Ben. *New Life Insurance Investment Advisor: Achieving Financial Security for You and Your Family through Today's Insurance Products.*2nd ed. New York: McGraw-Hill, 2001.
   Guide to how to analyze insurance products based on investment potential and financial returns. Provides guide to how to conduct research and determine the best products for various stages of life.

Hungelmann, Jack. *Insurance for Dummies.* Hoboken, NJ: Wiley, 2009.
   A practical guide about insurance focuses on finding the best health, life, home, and automobile policies; working through the claims process; finding the right health care plan; and evaluating the market for types of insurance policies.

Life and Health Insurance Foundation for Education (http://www.life happens.org).
   Provides practical advice to consumers and features an introduction to life insurance and information on the fundamentals of health insurance, life insurance, and long-term care insurance and how to find an agent or a company. Includes Insurance 101 videos.

Yahoo! Finance—Insurance (http://finance.yahoo.com/insurance).
   Features recent articles, information on how to save money on automobile insurance, expert opinion, calculators, and how-to guides: *Buying Life Insurance* and *Disability Income Insurance.*

DATA AND STATISTICS SOURCES

In addition to obtaining industry reports online from *Standard & Poor's NetAdvantage, Hoover's,* and *Mergent Online,* the following are industry-specific sources for the insurance industry.

A. M. Best (http://www.ambest.com).

A. M. Best, founded by Alfred M. Best in 1899, is a worldwide insurance rating and information agency. Publisher of *Best's Insurance Reports* (*Property/Casualty* and *Life/Health*) and the journal *Best's Review Magazine*. *Best's Insurance Reports* are available online and in print formats. The Online Financial Suite (http://www.ambest.com/sales/statement) allows access to financial data and ratings for insurance companies. Best's includes ratings for insurance companies from A++ (superior) to F (in liquidation) and S (suspended).

A. M. Best's Complete News Service: Real-Time, Daily, Weekly, Monthly

Provides news reports and ratings notifications in real time via BestWire. News about the industry and any credit rating alerts on a daily basis is provided through BestDay. News on a weekly basis is provided through Best Week and on a monthly basis through Best's Review.

Best's Aggregates and Averages. Print and online.

Contains aggregated information for life/health and property/casualty insurance. Includes information on balance sheet and summary of operations, quantitative analysis reports, key pages of the annual statement for the current year for property/casualty and life/health insurance, time series (property/casualty), and analysis of operations by line (life/health edition). Also provides company-specific data, including leading companies and group ranking of leading writers of property/casualty and life/health insurance.

Best's Life/Health Center (http://www3.ambest.com/lh/default.asp and http://www.ambest.com/sales/BIR/default.asp).

Provides access to a database to search financial information and ratings of insurance companies. The major print publication in the area of Life Health is the following:

Best's Insurance Reports: Life/Health. Oldwick, NJ: A. M. Best Co. Annual.

Provides top 100 U.S. company and 50 top Canadian company listings. Provides directory information for life/health insurance companies and features for each company an entry name, address, telephone, fax, email, website, Best's rating, Best's rating five-year summary, officers and directors, reviews of business, and North American Industry Classification System (NAICS).

Best's Property/Casualty Center (http://www3.ambest.com/pc/default.asp and http://www.ambest.com/sales/BIRPC/default.asp).

The online database allows the searching of property/casualty insurance companies and also provides the latest news on the insurance industry. The major print publication in the area of property/casualty insurance is the following:

Best's Insurance Reports: Property/Casualty. Oldwick, NJ: A. M. Best Co. Annual.

In addition to listing the top 100 companies and the top 50 in Canada, this annual directory lists insurance companies, and each entry includes name, address, Best's rating, five-year rating history, key financial indicators, officers and directors, rating rationale, where a company is licensed, reviews of business, and NAICS classification.

American Council of Life Insurers (http://www.acli.com/ACLI/Default NotLoggedIn.htm).
Trade association and publisher of the annual *Life Insurers Fact Book*, available in online format. The *Fact Book* provides statistics and information on trends in the life insurance industry and reviews industry trends for the year. Specific topics covered include assets, liabilities, income, expenditures, reinsurance, life insurance, and annuities. Features listings of the largest life insurers by various categories that include total assets, general account assets, separate account assets, and individual net life insurance premiums. Also features other online publications related to the life insurance industry, including a guide on how to purchase this type of insurance.

Fitch Insurance Ratings (http://www.fitchratings.com/web_content/product/ Fitch%20Research%20-%20Insurance%20Fact%20Sheet.pdf).
Online subscription service providing access to Fitch ratings of insurance companies. Fitch Research's insurance coverage includes life, health, property and casualty, and financial guaranty as well as reinsurance, securitization, and title and mortgage companies.

Health Decisions.org (http://www.healthdecisions.org).
Sponsored by America's Health Insurance Plans, provides news releases and links to vendor selection tools to locate health insurance plans, legislative news related to health care, and tools for consumers.

ISIS (Insurance Companies Worldwide) (http://eps.bvdep.com/en/ISIS.html).
Database providing information for 9,500 insurance companies worldwide from Bureau Van Dijk Electronic Publishing. Each company report includes name, address, phone, fax, website, status, reporting basis, Fitch account number, specialization (e.g., life or health), total assets, profit after tax, number of recorded subsidiaries, major business lines (e.g., property/casualty) and revenues, major geographic markets, balance sheet, income statement, names of subsidiaries (with revenue), stock prices (when applicable), and mergers and acquisitions. The Peer Report compares the insurance company with others in its peer group in terms of financials and ratio analyses. Interactive database allows for sorting and formatting data to create reports.

The Insurance Almanac. New York: Criterion Publishing. Annual (http:// www.criterioninsurancedirectory.com).
Directory of insurance marketing information on property and casualty companies; life, health, and accident companies; assigned risk plans and rating bureaus; state insurance officials; trade associations; and agents/ brokers,. Directory information includes list of name of company, address, telephone number, email, officers, and websites. Other information sources from this publisher include state and local directories and directory information in Excel spreadsheet format.

The Insurance Bar: A Select Directory of Prominent Lawyers Chosen with Particular Regard to Experience and Training in Insurance Practice plus Expert Services Providers. Cleveland, OH: Insurance Bar, Inc. Annual.

Directory of lawyers related to specific areas of insurance practice and specialization. Also contains directory information for claims services (claims adjusters), state insurance officials, state motor vehicle officials, and expert services providers, including appraisers and property. Each entry includes name, address, telephone, email, website, and description of services.

The Insurance Directory: The Guide to Companies in the U.K. London: Insurance Directory. Almanac.

Provides a review of the year in the British insurance industry, a directory of underwriters, a directory of insurance brokers and intermediaries, a geographical index, and a directory of trade insurance trade associations in the United Kingdom. The entry for each company includes name, address, website, number of employees, and key lines of business.

Insurance Information Institute (http://www.iii.org).

Aims to improve public understanding of insurance, what it does, and how it works. Insurance tools contains a directory of state insurance departments, insurance companies, and state organizations; auto crash test ratings; a glossary; and an "Ask the Expert" section. Publishes the *Insurance Handbook*, a guide to auto, home, life, disability, and business insurance, and features issue papers, a glossary, and directories. The "Insurance Topics" section lists topics that include property insurance, long-term care, and commercial auto. Within each topic there are links to basic articles (practical guides to specific topics) and backgrounders and research with more detailed information.

Insurance Institute for Highway Safety, Highway Loss Data Institute (http://www.iihs.org).

The Insurance Institute for Highway safety is "an independent, nonprofit, scientific and educational associations dedicated to reducing the losses . . . from crashes on the nation's highways" (website). The Highway Loss Data Institute "shares and supports this mission through scientific studies of insurance data representing the human and economic losses resulting from the ownership and operation of different types of vehicles and publishing insurance loss results by vehicle make and model" (website). Provides vehicle ratings data, consumer information, research and statistics (e.g., fatalities by year and insurance losses by make and model), and an insurance loss fact sheet.

Insure.com (http://www.insure.com).

For consumers, provides searchable database to locate the best price quotes for health insurance, car insurance, life insurance, home insurance, and other insurance. Also provides a glossary, insurance news releases, and tools, including calculators.

Life Insurance Marketing and Research Association (LIMRA) (http://www
.limra.com).
   Provides marketing research data on life insurance and annuities. Features
   statistics on sales and projections of sales on life insurance and annuities.
   Features online publications: *LIMRA MarketTrends Fact Book (United
   States)* and *LIMRA MarketTrends Fact Book (Canada)* and other publications
   that provide data on the performance of various markets, including long-
   term care insurance.

National Association of Insurance Commissioners and the Center for Insurance Policy and Research (http://www.naic.org)
   "The Mission of the NAIC is to assist state insurance regulators, individu-
   ally and collectively, in serving the public interest and achieving the following fundamental insurance regulatory goals . . . : promote the public
   interest; promote competitive markets; facilitate the fair and equitable
   treatment of insurance consumers; promote the reliability, solvency and
   financial solidity of insurance institutions; and support and improve state
   regulation of insurance" (website). Features the Consumer Information
   Source, containing financial data about insurance companies, how to file
   an insurance complaint, and aggregate consumer complaint reports.

Plunkett, Jack W. *Plunkett's Insurance Industry Almanac*. Houston: Plunkett
Research Annual. Annual (http://www.plunkettresearch.com).
   The stated purpose of the almanac is "to be a general source for researchers
   of all types." Contains an essay of the year's major trends in the insurance
 · industry (e.g., the continued rise in health care costs, mergers, and
   acquisitions), a glossary of terms, and the Insurance 300, the leading
   insurance companies from the United States and internationally. Each
   entry includes name, address, phone, fax, website, description of business activities, NAICS classification code, ranking within the specific
   company's industry group, financials (profits and sales), stock ticker
   symbol, and branches (if applicable).

Property Casualty Insurers Association of America (http://www.pciaa.net/
web/sitehome.nsf/main).
   Trade association representing companies in the property/casualty insurance market. Sponsors seminars and meetings, and members have access
   to publications, compliance guides, and statistical publications. The
   Greenbook is an annual reference guide to statistical information on the
   property casualty insurance industry. Statistics available in the Greenbook include operating results, premiums, and losses and expenses, plus
   miscellaneous auto and selected auto and crime data in downloadable
   Excel files.

Risk and Insurance Management Society, Inc. (http://www.rims.org/Pages/
Default.aspx).
   A nonprofit organization dedicated to "advancing the practice of risk man-
   agement" (website). Features webinars, information about conferences,
   continuing education, and resources, including *Risk Management
   Magazine*.

U.S. Census Bureau, Health Insurance Data (http://www.census.gov/hhes/
www/hlthins).
  The Census Bureau collects health insurance using three national surveys:
  the Current Population Survey's Annual Social and Economic Supplement (CPS ASEC), the American Community Survey, and the Survey of
  Income and Program Participation. The CPS ASEC collects and publishes
  health insurance data annually for national and state-level geographies.
  Among the statistics provided are those for health insurance coverage
  of children under 18 for 2008 and 2009, public coverage by sex and age,
  and private health insurance by sex and age.

U.S. Social Security Administration (http://www.ssa.gov).
  Features information about Medicare, featuring downloadable publications and information on how to apply online for disability benefits and
  how to request a Social Security statement.

Weiss Ratings Series http://www.weissratings.com/
  Provides ratings and advisory information for policyholders and potential
  policyholders. Weiss rates each company by measures of risk, reserve
  adequacy index, profitability index, liquidity index, and stability index.
  Ratings range from excellent (A) to failed (F). Each company listed
  includes name, address, telephone, fax, website, principal business, rating, net income, total assets, loss ratio, and data for companies that have
  changed ratings (upgrades or downgrades) since the last issue.

Weiss Ratings' Guide to Health Insurers (Formerly *The Street.com Ratings Guide to
  Health Insurers*). Amenia, NY: Grey House Publishing. Published quarterly (http://www.weissratings.com).
  Focuses on health insurance, including medical reimbursement insurers,
  managed health care, disability insurance, long-term care, and dental
  insurance. Also provides answers to questions about Medicare.

Weiss Ratings' Guide to Life and Annuity Insurance (Formerly *The Street.com Rating's Guide to Life and Annuity Insurers*). Amenia, NY: Grey House Publishing. Published quarterly (http://www.weissratings.com).
  Covers companies providing life and annuity insurance. Recommended
  for those considering the purchase of a life insurance policy, placing
  money in an annuity, or advising clients about insurance and annuities.

Weiss Ratings' Guide to Property and Casualty Insurers (Formerly *The Street.com
  Ratings' Guide to Property and Casualty Insurers*). Amenia, NY: Grey House
  Publishing. Published quarterly (http:www.weissratings.com).
  Covers property/casualty insurers and companies that provide insurance for
  home, business, automobile, compensation, property liability, and so on.

PERIODICAL INDEXES AND FULL-TEXT DATABASES

For insurance full-text articles and indexes and abstracts, recommended databases are *ABI/INFORM, Business Source Premier,*

Lexis/Nexis, and *ScienceDirect*. A database specifically for insurance is the following:

Insurance Periodicals Index (IPI) (EBSCO) (http://www.ebscohost.com/ academic/insurance-periodicals-index).
   IPI was formerly produced by the NILS Publishing Co., Inc., in cooperation with the Insurance and Employee Benefits Division of the Special Libraries Association. It is an index and abstract to approximately 200 leading insurance industry journals and magazines. Indexes and abstracts journals, some back to 1946, and features a controlled vocabulary of index terms. Indexes and abstracts nearly 200 of the most respected and widely read insurance industry journals and magazines. Coverage dates as far back as 1946 and features a controlled vocabulary of index terms that reflects current insurance industry terminology.

PERIODICALS AND NEWSPAPERS

In addition to consulting periodicals such as *Barron's* and the *Wall Street Journal*, specific insurance related publications include the following:

The Actuary (http://www.the-actuary.org.uk)
Annals of Actuarial Science (http://www.ingentaconnect.com/content/fia/aas)
Broker World (http://www.brokerworldmag.com/pages/index.php ?recordID=1)
Business Insurance (http://www.businessinsurance.com)
Health Insurance Underwriter (http://www.nahu.org/media/HIU/index.cfm)
Journal of Insurance Operations (http://www.jiops.com)
Journal of Risk and Insurance (http://www.wiley.com/bw/journal.asp ?ref=0022-4367)
National Underwriter: Life and Health (http://www.lifeandhealthinsurancenews .com/Pages/default.aspx)
National Underwriter: Property and Casualty (http://www.property-casualty .com/Pages/default.aspx)
Risk Analysis: An International Journal (http://www.blackwellpublishing.com/ journal.asp?ref=0272-4332)
Risk and Insurance (http://www.riskandinsurance.com)
Rough Notes Magazine (http://www.roughnotes.com/rnmagrenewal.htm)

A MAJOR SPECIAL LIBRARY FOR THE INSURANCE INDUSTRY

St. John's University, School of Risk Management. Davis Library (http:// www.stjohns.edu/academics/libraries/campus/davis).
   Located in downtown Manhattan, the Davis Library is a library that specializes in insurance information. Its mission statement is as follows:

"By collecting, organizing, preserving and making available published and unpublished resources about risk, insurance and actuarial studies, the Kathryn and Shelby Cullom Davis Library strives to advance the understanding of the insurance industry's history, analysis, management and business culture. The Library's goal is to provide these resources to create a unique prospective of the impact the insurance industry has had and will continue to have on the economic, political and cultural development of the United States and the world.

"As an ACADEMIC SPECIALTY library and repository, the Davis Library supports the academic needs of faculty and students in the St. John's University School of Risk Management , Insurance, and Actuarial Science.

"As a PRIVATE SPECIALTY library and repository, the Davis Library supports the information and knowledge acquisition needs of the risk, insurance and actuarial enterprise and its practitioners.

"As a SCHOLARLY, PRIVATE SPECIALTY library and repository, the Davis Library supports the research needs of the national and international scholarly community."

The Kathryn and Shelby Cullom Davis Library carries out it's mission and vision by fulfilling its role as a key facilitator of information access for research, user-centered learning and information literacy in the areas of risk, hazards, insurance and actuarial science." (website).

11

Management and Small Business Management and Entrepreneurship

MANAGEMENT

Management is defined as "all that is involved in making the most effective use of available resources, whether in the form of machines, money or people" (*Concise Dictionary of Business Management*). The functions of management are planning (objective setting and determining a course of action), organizing (developing an organizational structure), leading (leadership in implementing organizational objectives), and controlling (establishing performance standards and measuring them against an organization's standards).

Topics of study in management include organizational behavior, management science and operations research, industrial psychology entrepreneurship, organizational culture, organizational learning, training and development, and leadership.

This chapter will focus on resource materials for management practitioners, faculty, and students. Since the study of small business management is often part of programs in business administration and there is interest in information in how to set up and run a small business, this chapter also concentrates on entrepreneurship.

Encyclopedias and Dictionaries

Encyclopedia of Leadership. George R. Goethals, General Editor. Thousand Oaks, CA: Sage Publications, 2004. 4 volumes.

Features approximately 400 entries that address leadership theories, leadership practices, and the effects of leadership in the world. According to the preface, "this Encyclopedia addresses questions: What is a great leader? What is leadership? What is a great follower? How does someone become a leader? What are the types of leadership? How can leadership theories help us understand contemporary situations? How can I learn to be good and perhaps even a great leader? The Encyclopedia contains entries related to leadership in various areas: political, business and management, religious, etc. The entries are alphabetical, but the editors group entries within broader categories in their Readers Guide." For instance, under the category of "Business," researchers can locate articles on management, small business, Jack Welch, Ralph Nader, John D. Rockefeller, Alfred Sloan, trust busting, the labor movement, and Ray Kroc, among others. Also provides a bibliography of significant books on leadership.

Encyclopedia of Management. Edited by Marilyn M. Helms. 4th ed. Detroit: Gale Group, 2000.
Features an alphabetical list of entries, with an index and cross-references. Contributors to each essay/entry are college and university faculty members, consultants, and librarians. A guide is included to "functional area readings" where researchers can focus in on only the articles that deal with a specific aspect of management. For instance, those researching management science and operations research will find a list of entries that includes management science, inventory management, statistics, constraints, models and modeling, and object-oriented programming. Essays are detailed and feature references for further reading.

Heery, Edmund, and Mike Noon. *A Dictionary of Human Resource Management.* New York: Oxford University Press, 2001.
Defines terms related to the field of human resource management. Alphabetical arrangement of terms with a classification grouping in Appendix 1 (e.g., terms under the category "Employee Representation" include block vote, general union, and industrial union). Appendix 2 contains abbreviations and acronyms. Also provides cross-references. Among terms defined are employee relations, layoff, lateral career moves, organizational culture, and leadership.

Statt, David A. *The Routledge Dictionary of Business Management.* 3rd ed. London: Routledge, 2004.
Contains concise definitions of terms and also entries for noted individuals in management. Covers terms including corporate strategy, fifth discipline, flexible time, burnout, and change agent.

Directory

The Directory of Executive & Professional Recruiters. Peterborough, NH: Kennedy Information, Inc. Annual. Print and online formats (http://www.kennedyinfo.com/).

Directory of recruiters for those seeking jobs in the corporate world. Divided into categories of retainer recruiting firms and contingency recruiting firms. Indexes make it possible to search by job title, job function, or position; specific industry categories; recruiter specialties; geographic location; and names of firms. Each entry contains name, address, phone, fax, email, Web address, key contacts, salary ultimate (lowest salary for positions handled), specialty areas, and branch offices.

Handbook

21st Century Management: A Reference Handbook. Edited by Charles Wankel. Los Angeles: Sage Publications, 2008. 2 volumes.

According to its editor, this source "provides clear and useful discussion by scholars around the world of 100 of the key issues and topics that managers are confronting in the 21st century." Topics include entrepreneurship, contemporary issues of business and society and government, managing the global enterprise, sustainability and the natural environment, strategy in a fast and networked world, operations management with new technologies in a global context, organizing in the post-9/11 world, human resources as a key strategic factor, organizational behavior, leadership without boundaries, information and knowledge with mobility and ethics, organizational development and change in the twenty-first century, and nonbusiness organizations: new perspectives. Each category contains a series of essays by experts in the field. For instance, essays within the category of entrepreneurship in the twenty-first century include "Women Entrepreneurs," "Corporate Entrepreneurship," and "High Technology Entrepreneurship." Authors of essays are based at universities throughout the world. Bibliographic references are provided with each essay.

Mission Statements

Abrahams, Jeffrey. *The Mission Statement Book: 301 Corporate Mission Statements from America's Top Companies.* Berkeley, CA: Ten Speed Press, 1999.

Part I of this source is a description and analysis of a mission statement, what it is used for, why it is important to have one, which elements make up the mission statement, and how missions differ from one another, and part II contains the mission statements themselves. According to the author, a mission statement is defined as "an enduring statement of purpose for an organization that defines the scope of its operations and product and market terms, and reflects its values and priorities." Each entry (from the actual company mission statement) includes vision, corporate objectives, address, and industry category.

Biographical Information

The Biographical Dictionary of Management. General Editor: Morgen Witzel,
General Editor. Bristol: Thoemmes Press, 2001. 2 volumes.
  Source that focuses on not only management as it is in contemporary times
  but also the historical aspects of the development of management. Main
  entries are alphabetically arranged and contain approximately 600 entries
  representing thinkers and practitioners of management. A chronological
  list organizes entries by dates of birth. Also includes diverse coverage.
  Contains entries for, among others, William Randolph Hearst, Confucius,
  Aaron Montgomery Ward, Conrad Hilton, Joseph Schumpeter, Coco
  Chanel, Edsel Ford, John Kenneth Galbraith, Rosabeth Moss Kanter, Peter
  Drucker, Ted Turner, and Berry Gordy. Each entry is approximately two
  to three pages and contains bibliographical references.

The International Directory of Business Biographies. Neil Schlager, Editor. Detroit:
St. James Press, an imprint of Thomson Gale, 2005. 4 volumes.
  Profiles over 600 prominent businesspeople around the world. This source
  is designed for use by management students, librarians, faculty, and historians. Arrangement is alphabetical by surname and includes within
  each entry a fact box (e.g., birth and death dates, family information,
  work history, and publications), the main text of the article, bibliographic
  citations, and cross-references. Among those profiled are Jeff Bezos, Warren Buffett, Bill Gates, David Geffen, Martha Stewart, Donald Trump,
  Steve Jobs, Oprah Winfrey, Jack Welch, and Ted Turner.

Krismann, Carol. *Encyclopedia of Women in Business: From Colonial Times to
Present.* Westport, CT: Greenwood Press, 2005. 2 volumes.
  Entries are listed alphabetically. Source includes not only biographical
  entries but also terms (e.g., affirmative action) related to women in business. Profiles feature biographies of each woman profiled plus a list of
  sources for further reading. Among the women profiled are Oprah Winfrey, Martha Stewart, Ruth Handler, and Sylvia Porter. A chronology of
  the history of women in business is also featured.

Government Agencies Related to Employees Rights

Managers and their employees need to keep current on information
related to equal opportunity employment and fair labor practices.
The following agencies are core agencies for employee rights.

U.S. Equal Employment Opportunity Commission (EEOC) (http://www.eeoc
.gov).
  The EEOC is responsible for compliance and enforcement activities regarding equal employment opportunity. Contains news reports, laws and
  regulation, guides on how to file a complaint, outreach and education,
  and litigation statistics.

National Labor Relations Board (http://www.nlrb.gov).
> An independent federal agency that safeguards employees' rights to organize and determine to have unions as their bargaining representative. Website contains the text of the National Labor Relations Act and publishes manuals and guides and rules and regulations.

Management Associations

American Management Association (http://www.amanet.org).
> Provides training programs, books related to various aspects of management, working papers, corporate on-site solutions, webcasts, and podcasts. Publishes series of guides and handbooks of management for both practitioners and students.

The Conference Board (http://www.conference-board.org).
> The mission of the Conference Board is to "to provide the world's leading organizations with the practical knowledge they need to improve their performance and better serve society" (website). Publisher of special reports related to topics of management, including corporate leadership, high-performing organizations, organizational chart collection, and human capital. Publications are of value to both practitioners and faculty and students of business.

Online Full-Text Databases and Periodical Indexes

Management, small business, and entrepreneurship periodical articles are located via searches of the following databases: *ABI/INFORM*, *Business Source Premier*, and *ScienceDirect*. For articles related to organizational psychology and behavior, researchers should consult *PsycInfo* (available directly from the American Psychological Association and also through the vendor EBSCOhost).

The following are major journals of management:

Academy of Management Journal (http://journals.aomonline.org/amj)
Harvard Business Review (http://hbr.org)
Journal of Management (http://jom.sagepub.com)
Journal of Management Studies (http://www.wiley.com/bw/journal.asp?ref=0022-2380)
Journal of Organizational Behavior (http://onlinelibrary.wiley.com/journal/10.1002/(ISSN)1099-1379)
Management Science (http://mansci.journal.informs.org)
Strategic Management Journal (http://onlinelibrary.wiley.com/journal/10.1002/(ISSN)1097-0266)

SMALL BUSINESS MANAGEMENT AND ENTREPRENEURSHIP

A small business is privately owned and operated and has a small number of employees and a relatively low volume of sales. Small business range from hair salons to restaurants to convenience stores. An entrepreneur owns and operates and assumes the risk for the small business. A franchise is a type of business where an individual is given a license to run a company and agrees to use the franchisor's name, products, services, selling, distribution, and so on. Examples of franchises include McDonald's, Kentucky Friend Chicken, and Midas.

Sources related to small business management range from how-to guides, sample business plans, franchise opportunities, and agencies that offer assistance (e.g., training and financing).

Encyclopedia

Encyclopedia of Small Business. Edited by Arsan J. Darnay and Monique D. Magee. 3rd ed. Detroit: Thomson Gale, 2007. 2 volumes.
    Intended for students of business, entrepreneurs, and future business owners, this resource features entries related to various aspects of small business. The approximately 695 entries are listed alphabetically with cross-references. Included are entries for equipment leasing, selling a business, a multicultural workforce, and business hours. Entries are detailed with bibliographical references.

Directories

Directory of Mail Order Catalogs: A Comprehensive Guide to Consumer Mail Order Catalog Companies. Millerton, NY: Grey House Publishing, Annual (http://www.greyhouse.com/marketing.htm).
    Covers approximately 9,000 consumer catalog companies in the categories of products/services, including travel, office products, toys and games, clothing, health and personal care, baby products, home furnishings, food and beverage, and sporting equipment. Each entry provides information on name, address, telephone, fax, email, website, product lines, sales, officers, years in business, and catalog frequency and price.

Franchise Opportunities Guide. Washington, DC: International Franchise Association. Published twice annually.
    Guide to franchise opportunities, with contact information, company details, qualifications, and funding needed to purchase franchise. The International Franchise Association's website (http://www.franchise.org) contains a searchable database for locating franchise opportunities,

contains key definitions, and provides guidance to those wishing to buy a franchise and how to establish a franchised business.

National Minority and Women-Owned Business Directories. Minneapolis: Diversity Information Resources, Inc. Annual.

Arranged alphabetically by classifications (e.g., apparel and textiles) and contains a table of North American Industry Classification System classifications and a key word index. Each entry includes name and address, telephone number, fax, email, website, a description of the business, number of employees, sales, and ownership classification (e.g., Native American).

Small Business Sourcebook: The Entrepreneur's Resource. Detroit: Gale Cengage Learning, 1983–. 2 volumes.

Annotated guide to over 25,000 listings of sources related to small business start-up, development, and growth. Information presented is organized within the following sections: "Small Business Profiles" (arranged alphabetically by industry categories, containing start-up information, organizations, associations, reference works, periodicals, and so on), "General Small Business Topics" (containing associations, books, periodicals, articles, pamphlets, and so on), "State Listings" (government, academic, and commercial agencies and select coverage of relevant publications), and "Federal Government Assistance." Also includes a glossary of small business terms and a guide to publishers.

Guides

Ramsey, Dan, and Judy Ramsey. *The Everything Guide to Running a Retail Store.* Avon, MA: Adams Media, 2010.

Designed for those considering opening their own store, contains Retailing 101 (with key definitions), deciding on a type of retail store, whether to franchise, financial considerations, the business plan, selecting a location, store layout, hiring employees, accounting, and expanding the business. An appendix features a glossary of terms and a directory of key agencies and their websites.

Solie-Johnson, Kris. *How to Set Up Your Own Small Business.* Sherwood, MN: American Institute of Small Business, 2009. 2 volumes.

Presents practical advice on setting up and running a business, including advice on how to write a business plan; financial, accounting, and legal considerations; and marketing and sales management. Features sample forms and a glossary of terms.

Business Plans

Business Plans Handbook: A Compilation of Actual Business Plans Developed by Businesses throughout North America. Detroit: Thomson Gale. Volume 1,

1994–. Also available in ebook format through Gale Virtual Reference Library (http://www.gale.cengage.com/servlet/GvrlSeriesList?region =9&imprint=000&titleCode=EBK78&msg=ma&page=1).

Series of volumes contain business plans actually written by entrepreneurs seeking financing for their businesses. Arranged by services/industries and within each category contains a list of companies' business plans. Each business plan contains name address, executive summary, growth strategy, company history, operations, products and services, market analysis, financial analysis, advertising, and business strategy. Helpful as models for entrepreneurs who wish to obtain financing and to students of business learning about entrepreneurship.

Government Agencies, Organizations and Associations

Entrepreneur.com (http://www.entrepreneur.com).
Website for *Entrepreneur Magazine,* provides multitude of resources for present and prospective entrepreneurs. Among its features are "Starting a Business" (including a guide to specific types of businesses and reports on why businesses succeed and fail), "Franchises" (trends, top franchises within various industries, and links to franchises for sale), "Management" (advice on running a business), and "Business Opportunities" (browse by category).

International Franchise Association (http://www.franchise.org).
Offers assistance to present and future franchisors and franchisees. Offers book materials with directories of opportunities and how-to guides.

National Franchisee Association (https://www.nfabk.org).
Designed to offer support to the franchisee community at large. Specializes in support of Burger King as well as franchised restaurants.

Service Corps of Retired Executives (SCORE) (http://www.score.org).
SCORE "mentors to America's small business, is a nonprofit association dedicated to educating entrepreneurs and helping small business start, grow and succeed nationwide. SCORE is a resource partner with the U.S. Small Business Administration (SBA)" (website). Mentors are retired and working executives and business owners, and approximately 13,000 volunteer their time to SCORE. Provides links to templates and guides and also features podcasts and workshops. Also provides email alerts and the newsletters *SCORE eNews* and *SCORE ExpertANSWERS.* Allows selection of mentors by searchable "Find a Mentor Now" database.

U.S. Small Business Administration (SBA) (http://www.sba.gov).
A key resource for business owners and entrepreneurs and those interested in starting a small business, the SBA was "created in 1953 as an independent agency of the federal government to aid, counsel, assist and protect the interests of small business concerns, to preserve free competitive enterprise and to maintain and strengthen the overall economy of our nation"

(website). Features free virtual training courses, e-newsletters, and a frequently-asked-questions section and is a source of counseling and guidance, financial assistance, disaster assistance, and information about law/regulations. Of value to neophytes is the SBA's Start Up Guide (http://www.sba.gov/smallbusinessplanner/plan/getready/serv_sbplanner_stguide.html).

United States Association for Small Business and Entrepreneurship (http://usasbe.org).
The "leading voice in entrepreneurship research, teaching, and application" (website). Features Web links for entrepreneurship educators.

Journals

Black Enterprise Magazine (http://www.blackenterprise.com)
Entrepreneur Magazine (http://www.entrepreneur.com)
Franchise Times Magazine (http://www.franchisetimes.com)
Franchising World (http://www.franchise.org/defaultindustry.aspx)
Inc. Magazine (http://www.inc.com)
Journal of Small Business (http://www.wiley.com/bw/journal.asp?ref=0047-2778)
Journal of Small Business and Entrepreneurship (http://www.jsbe.com)
Wall Street Journal (section on resources for entrepreneurs) (http://online.wsj.com/public/page/news-small-business-marketing.html)

12

Marketing and Advertising

MARKETING

Marketing is defined by the American Marketing Association as "the activity, set of institutions, and processes for creating, communication, delivering and exchanging offerings that have value for customers, clients, partners and society at large."

According to the classic definitions of marketing in various dictionaries and in textbooks, marketing is comprised of the "four Ps": product, price, place, and promotion: "the selection and development of the product; determination of price, selection and design of distribution channels (place), and all aspects of generating or enhancing demand for the product . . . (promotion)" (*Dictionary of Marketing Terms*, 3rd ed).

Resources for marketing include dictionaries of encyclopedias, directories, statistics, and data sources for marketing research.

Encyclopedias and Dictionaries

IEBM Encyclopedia of Marketing. Edited by Michael J. Baker. London: International Thomson Business Press, 1999.
  Arranged within broad topics: the nature and scope of marketing, the theoretical foundation, marketing management, the marketing mix, marketing in practice, and special topics. Within each broad topic, specific articles are included. For instance, "Marketing in Practice" contains articles/entries: commodity marketing, business marketing, franchising, marketing of services, exporting, global marketing, marketing ethics, and strategic marketing for nonprofit organizations. Extensive bibliographical citations are included.

Imber, Jane, and Betsy-Ann Toffler. *Dictionary of Marketing Terms*. 3rd ed. Hauppauge, NY: Barron's Business Guides, 2000.

Contains definitions of terms and organizations related to marketing with an appendix of abbreviations and acronyms.

Gale Encyclopedia of E-Commerce. Edited by Jane A. Malonis. Farmington Hills, MI: Gale Group, 2002.
  Features profiles of pioneering companies and individuals who are seen as being on the forefront of the e-commerce revolution. Features entries for individuals, including Bill Gates, and companies, among which are America Online and Altavista.

Lewis, Barbara R. and Dale Littler. *The Blackwell Encyclopedic Dictionary of Marketing.* Cambridge, MA: Blackwell Publishers, 1997.
  Contains definitions of terms among which are direct marketing, telemarketing, retail buying, and reference groups. Features cross references and bibliographical references with each entry.

Mercer, David. *Marketing: The Encyclopedic Dictionary.* Malden, MA: Blackwell, 1999.
  Encyclopedia contains entries for terminology and concepts in marketing and is designed for practitioners, students, and faculty.

Ostrow, Rona. *The Fairchild Dictionary of Retailing.* 2nd ed. New York: Fairchild, 2009.
  Provides approximately 10,000 entries related to retailing, with cross-references. Designed for students and faculty in schools of business and for practitioners.

Wiley Encyclopedia of International Marketing. Jagdish Sheth and Naresh Malhotra, Editors in Chief. Hoboken, NJ: Wiley, 2011. 6 volumes. Available in print and online formats.
  An international guide to marketing concepts and application comprised of six volumes: volume 1: *Marketing Strategy*; volume 2: *Marketing Research*; volume 3: *Consumer Behavior*; volume 4: *Advertising and Integrated Communication*; volume 5: *Product Innovation and Management*; and volume 6: *International Marketing*. Entries range from brief definitions to short essays. Contains cross-references.

Yadin, Daniel. *The International Dictionary of Marketing: Over 2000 Professional Terms and Techniques.* Milford, CT: Kogan Page, 2002.
  Defines terms and with each concept includes the "connotation." For instance, for "deadline," three italicized words are included—"advertising, public relations, publishing"—which indicates that "deadline" is commonly used in advertising, public relations, and publishing.

Directories

The Direct Marketing Market Place. New Providence, NJ: National Register. Annual (http://www.dirmktgplace.com).
  Directory of direct marketers, service firms, and suppliers. Provides names, addresses, fax numbers, gross sales, advertising budget, and so on.

The Green Book (American Marketing Association, New York Chapter) (http:// www.greenbook.org). Also available in print.

Searchable database to locate marketing research companies and focus group facilities. The print directories are arranged in two volumes: volume 1: *Worldwide Directory of Marketing Research Companies and Services*, and volume 2: *Worldwide Directory of Focus Group Companies and Services*. Each entry includes name, address, telephone, email, website, professional affiliations, name of president/owner/principal, and a description of the market research company or focus group. Online database allows searching by market research methodology, type of service, industry, or audience.

Data Sources for Marketing Research

Research of specific markets for product and service lines provides researchers (practitioners at a company or business faculty and their students) with reports on the competition and/or opportunities available for new product/service lines. The reports also show which segments of the population use the products/services. It should be noted that current reports can be very costly and are generally directed to marketing research professionals, but earlier editions may be available at discounted prices for business schools. There are several databases that specialize in market studies: *Business Source Premier*, and *Market Research Reports* (http://web.ebscohost.com/bsi/publication?vid=2&hid=7 &sid=0c376014-a54c-409e-b541-96480b769987%40sessionmgr13). Select "Business Searching Interface" to locate selected *Datamonitor* reports on various industries. Search by key word or browse by industries: banking finance and insurance, high tech, industry and manufacturing, energy, business, and area studies.

Datamonitor (http://www.datamonitor.com).

Internationally focused source of research reports on various companies, industries, services, and products. Print and nonprint formats available. Categories include automotive, financial services, consumer packaged goods, pharmaceuticals and health care, and retailing.

European Marketing Data and Statistics. Chicago: Euromonitor International. Annual.

Provides marketing data for European countries. This work is arranged in 24 chapters presenting data that include advertising expenditures, consumer market size, household profiles, and economic indicators.

European Marketing Forecasts. Chicago: Euromonitor International. Annual.

Marketing forecasts for European countries. This work is arranged in several sections. Section 1 contains European marketing forecasts, including projections for demographics, economics, expenditures, and housing and households. The remaining sections contain statistics on various goods and services, such as beverages, clothing and footwear, and consumer electronics.

Frost & Sullivan (http://www.frost.com).
Provides industries and market studies for areas of: aerospace and defense, automotive and transportation, chemicals, materials and food, electronics and security, health care, industrial automation and process control, measurement and instrumentation, and energy and power systems. Focuses on current and emerging trends in various industries, products, and services.

IBIS World (http://www.ibisworld.com).
Reports by expert analysts cover 700 different market segments. Internationally focused coverage includes accommodation and food services, retail trade, manufacturing, health care, utilities, real estate, and information. Within each category are specific reports so that researchers can locate reports on casino hotels in the United States and single-location full-service restaurants, among other reports.

International Marketing Data and Statistics. Chicago: Euromonitor International. Annual.
Provides marketing statistics for the United States and Canada, North America, Latin American countries, Asia/Pacific nations, countries in Africa and the Middle East, and Australia and New Zealand. Section 1 consists of geographical information about each country, emphasizing economic, social, and political issues. The 23 other sections cover data including advertising expenditures, consumer market sizes, and household profiles.

International Marketing Forecasts. Chicago: Euromonitor International. Annual.
Presents data projecting statistics in most socioeconomic categories (for countries outside Europe) for the next 14 years for a majority of goods and services.

Market Research.com (http://www.marketresearch.com).
International focus. Features reports by research specialists and features categories: consumer goods, food and beverage, heavy industry, service industries, technology and media, and marketing and market research (including demographics). Within categories are specific reports, including an industry report on street vendors in the United States, fast-food eating places in China, and Indian fast-food market analysis.

Plunkett Research Ltd. (http://www.plunkettresearch.com/loginlink.aspx).
Print and nonprint products feature reports on specific products, services, and industries in addition to demographics. Covers reports in the categories of automotive, retailing, entertainment and media, transportation, wireless, and so on.

The Snapshots Series (ProQuest) (http://www.proquest.com/assets/literature/
products/databases/the_snapshots_series.pdf).
  Offers market data for various products and services. International in
  focus, covering over 30 industries in 26 countries. Allows libraries to purchase the entire database or select reports by region. Designed for students of business administration.

Regulation of Marketing

The following are agencies that protect consumers from unfair marketing practices by companies and that provide information about
unsafe products and promote the interests of the consumer.

Consumer Product Safety Commission (http://cpsc.gov).
  Alerts consumers to hazardous and unsafe products. Develops uniform
  safety standards for products.

U.S. Federal Communications Commission (FCC) (http://www.fcc.gov).
  The FCC is "charged with regulating interstate and international communications by radio, television, wire, satellite and cable. The FCC's jurisdiction covers the 50 states, the District of Columbia, and U.S. possessions"
  (website). The FCC investigates false advertising, among other issues.

U.S. Federal Trade Commission (FTC) (http://www.ftc.gov/index.shtml).
  The FTC "is the only federal agency with both consumer protection and
  competition jurisdiction in broad sectors of the economy" (website).

U.S. Food and Drug Administration (http://www.fda.gov).
  Provides product information related to food, drugs, medical devices, cos-
  metics, vaccines, and animal and veterinary products and provides news
  about recalls and safety alerts.

Marketing: Data Sources (Media Rates)

Sales and Marketing Management (http://www.salesandmarketing.com).
  "Survey of Buying Power" is a special supplement of Sales and Marketing
  Management that contains rankings of metropolitan statistical areas by
  population, retail sales, buying power, and so on. Features current and
  projected statistics and provides a glossary of terms used.

Standard Rate and Data Service (http://www.srds.com/library) Print and online formats.
  Provides access to the most current database of media rates, including
  media types: print, broadcast, newspaper, direct marketing, and online.
  Lists not only rates but also circulation and selected demographics and
  market information for metropolitan areas and countries.

Market Share Analysis

Market Share Reporter: An Annual Compilation of Reported Market Share Data on Companies, Products, and Services. Detroit, MI: Gale Cengage Learning. Annual. 2 volumes. Also online on Gale Directory Library (http://www.gale.cengage.com/pdf/facts/MarketShareRepOnGDL.pdf).

Market share analysis is the study of a company's sales as compared to its competitors in an industry. For products and services, the amount spent by consumers on a specific product or service as is compared with competitive brands within the same category. In addition to the entries, also contains indexes by source (of the data), place-names, products, services, names and issues index, company index, and brand index. Each entry contains the heading, both Standard Industry Classification (SIC) and North American Industry Classification System (NAICS) codes, and source of data. For instance, researchers can locate the top manufacturers of various products.

Marketing: Data Sources (Demographics)

Consumer USA (http://www.euromonitor.com/Consumer_USA).

Consumer USA provides volume and value market size data in historical and forecasted (2009–2013) time series for over 330 consumer markets. Provides data on manufacture and brand shares data for all major consumer goods. Detailed data on sales of products.

Editor and Publisher Market Guide. Irvine, CA: Editor and Publisher. Annual. (http://www.editorandpublisher.com/Resources/PublicationDeatails.aspx?PublicationID=10).

Uses 91 variables to project the year's retail sales, income levels, and demographic composition of the United States and Canada. Editor and Publisher's forecasting model is based on economic indicators from the Department of Commerce, the Bureau of Economic Analysis, state data centers, and chambers of commerce. Features market ranking tables with year-end projections for every metropolitan statistical area and the top 250 counties and cities with daily newspapers. Data collected in the ranking tables include population, disposable income, and total retail sales by category.

Online Marketing and E-Commerce

Plunkett's E-Commerce and Internet Business Almanac, by Jack W. Plunkett. Houston: Plunkett Research Ltd. Annual (http://plunkettresearch.com. Also includes database on CD-ROM.

Contains analysis of major trends affecting the e-commerce and Internet business, statistics, and the E-Commerce 450, the top e-commerce companies. Each profile includes name, address, financials, website, growth plans, contacts, brands/divisions/affiliates, and salaries and benefits.

Zimmerman, Jan. *Web Marketing for Dummies.* Hoboken, NJ: Wiley, 2009
Guide to planning and building effective websites and features illustrations of sample websites. Covers advertising, legal considerations, working with shopping search engines, keeping statistics of users, and using social networking sites.

Major Marketing Organizations

American Marketing Association (http://www.marketingpower.com/Pages/default.aspx).
Features a resource library, career guidance, a marketing resource directory, a guide to social media and marketing research, an e-newsletter, and webcasts.

Direct Marketing Association (http://www.the-dma.org/index.php).
For people doing direct marketing. Includes bookstore, news reports, upcoming events and seminars, research, and full-text white papers.

Periodical Indexes and Full-Text Databases

For marketing and advertising articles (full text) and indexes and abstracts, recommended databases are *ABI/INFORM*, *Business Source Premier*, *LEXIS/NEXIS*, and *ScienceDirect*.

Journals

Consumer Reports (http://www.consumerreports.org/cro/index.htm)
Industrial Marketing Management (http://www.elsevier.com/wps/find/journaldescription.cws_home/505720/description#description)
International Journal of Research in Marketing (http://www.elsevier.com/wps/find/journaldescription.cws_home/505550/description)
Journal of Marketing Education (http://jmd.sagepub.com)
Journal of Marketing Research (http://www.marketingpower.com/About AMA/Pages/AMA%20Publications/AMA%20Journals/Journal%20of%20Marketing%20research/JournalofMarketingresearch.aspx)
Marketing Research (http://www.marketingpower.com/AboutAMA/Pages/AMA%20Publications/AMA%20Magazines/Marketing%20Research/MarketingResearch.aspx)
Sales and Marketing Management (http://www.salesandmarketing.com)

ADVERTISING

Advertising is a major marketing tool, designed to influence consumers to purchase certain products or services—it is a key part of one of marketing's "four Ps": promotion. Advertisements promote a product or service via media that include printed newspapers and magazines, company websites, digital or print catalogs, radio, and television. The following are key sources in advertising research.

Encyclopedias and Dictionaries

The Advertising Age Encyclopedia of Advertising. Edited by John McDonough and Karen Egolf. New York: Fitzroy Dearborn Publishers, 2003. 3 volumes.
Illustrated encyclopedia of advertising with entries for terminology (e.g., classified advertising), specific products and services (e.g., coffee), companies (listing their advertising agencies), biographies, advertising agencies, and trade associations. Illustrations include portraits of those profiled in biographies and illustrations from commercials and advertisements. Bibliography provided with each entry.

Encyclopedia of Consumer Brands. Detroit: St. James Press, 1994. 3 volumes.
Features profiles of products that have been "leaders" in their respective business categories, among which are Gatorade, Pepsi Cola, Miracle Whip, and Domino Sugar. Discusses the product origins and advertising strategies used to promote these products. Products featured cover the categories of consumable products, personal products, and durable goods.

Encyclopedia of Major Marketing Campaigns. Edited by Thomas Riggs. Detroit: Gale Group, 2000. 2 volumes.
Profiles 500 of "the most notable advertising and marketing initiatives of the twentieth century" (preface). Lists companies alphabetically (and products, services, and name of promotion listed under each company's name). For instance, below "Avis Rent a Car," the slogan "We Try Harder" is listed (regarding the name of the advertising slogan). Under each company, there is an overview of the company itself, historical context, target market, competition, marketing strategy, and outcome of the promotion. An illustration of the ad(s) is included, as is a bibliography for further reading.

Room, Adrian. *Encyclopedia of Corporate Names Worldwide.* Jefferson, NC: McFarland, 2002.
Contains entries for over 5,500 commercial names, including corporations, product and trade names, and the origins and a brief description. Entries include Greyhound, Burlington, Burger King, Bullock's, Donna Karan, Mastercard, Mattel, Scribner, and Seagram. After the name in parentheses,

the nature of the product, corporation, or brand is provided, for instance, "Scrabble (board game)."

Room, Adrian. *NTC's Dictionary of Trade Name Origins.* Lincolnwood, IL: NTC Business Books, 1991.
   Contains alphabetical dictionary of trade names, with name of company that produced product, history of the product, how the name was derived, and a description of the product. Includes familiar product names, such as Coca-Cola, Coke, Honda, Marlboro, Polaroid, Playtex, and Listerine.

Weichman, Jack G. *NTC's Dictionary of Advertising.* 2nd ed. Lincolnwood, IL: National Textbook Company, 1993.
   Provides definition of key terms related to advertising as well as entries for organizations and associations.

Directories

Advertising Redbooks.com (LexisNexis) (http://www.ana.net). Also available in print format.
   Profiles both advertising agencies and advertisers. For agencies, 15,000 U.S. and international agencies are covered. Each entry includes name, address, telephone, email, fax, website, leading executives, number of employees, year founded, its specialization, annual billings broken down by media, and current and new accounts. For advertisers, covers over 25,000 U.S. companies and international companies that spend a minimum of $200,000 on advertising. Each entry includes name, address, telephone number, email, website, business description, personnel, approximate advertising expenditures, the advertising agency, and a list of brands handled by the agency and the executive(s) responsible for the company's account. The online database allows searching by various parameters. For agencies, search by market specialization and agency type, and for advertisers, search by NAICS or SIC or by industry group or brand name. Allows searching by location for both advertisers and advertising agencies.

The Brands and Their Companies (http://www.gale.cengage.com/pdf/facts/ BrandsTheirCo.pdf). Also available through Dialog. Online and print formats.
   Covers over 400,000 consumer brands and 115,000 manufacturers, importers, and distributors. Search by specific name brand to locate the company that produced it. Contact information is provided for each company. Also provides data on companies that have gone out of business and products no longer produced.

Online Archive of Historical Ads: Ad *Access, Duke University Libraries, John W. Hartman Center for Sales, Advertising and Marketing History (http://library.duke.edu/digitalcollections/adaccess).

Image database of over 7,000 advertisements from the United States and Canada from 1911 to 1955. Concentrates on the main subject areas: radio, television, transportation, beauty and hygiene, and World War II. Browsable and searchable content.

Biography

The Ad Men and Women: A Biographical Dictionary of Advertising. Edited by Edd Applegate. Westport, CT: Greenwood Press, 1994.
Series of biographical profiles of key ad men and women. Articles are signed and include a bibliography for further reading and a list of the clients' most notable campaigns. Among those included are David Ogilvy, Volney B. Palmer (the nation's first ad man and father of today's advertising agency), Walter Dill Scott, George Batten, Marion Harper, Jane Trahey, and Francis Wayland Ayer.

Major Advertising Organizations

American Academy of Advertising (http://www.aaasite.org).
For the advertising professional, academic, and student, this association fosters research endeavors and promotes a forum for the exchange of ideas. Publishes the *Journal of Advertising*, the *Journal of Interactive Advertising*, and the annual conference *Proceedings, the Academy.* Also disseminates research findings and scholarly contributions related to advertising.

American Advertising Federation (AAF) (http://www.aaf.org).
The oldest national advertising trade organization, the AAF acts as the "Unifying Voice for Advertising." AAF initiatives include a national conference, an Advertising Hall of Fame, the ADDY Awards, and scholarship and internship opportunities and publishes *Interact*, an online newsletter.

American Association of Advertising Agencies (http://www.aaaa.org/Pages/default.aspx).
National association for advertising agencies. Sponsors awards and events, including Advertising Week. Features news reports, transcripts of speeches, research reports, and position papers.

Association of National Advertisers (http://www.ana.net).
Organized to "to safeguard and advance the interests of advertisers and consumers" (website). Provides its membership with research reports and papers, conferences and meetings, webinars, and advocacy initiatives and is the publisher of *ANA Magazine*.

Periodical Indexes and Full-Text Databases

See the "Marketing" section.

Journals

Advertising Age (http://adage.com)
AdWeek (http://www.adweek.com/aw/index.jsp)
Brandweek (http://www.brandweek.com/bw/index.jsp)
International Journal of Advertising (http://www.internationaljournalof
    advertising.com)
Journal of Advertising (http://www.mesharpe.com/mall/results1.asp?acr=joa)
Journal of Advertising Education (http://www.aaasite.org/Journal_of_Ad
    _Education.html)
Journal of Interactive Advertising (http://jiad.org)

13

Careers and Job Hunting

The two major milestones in a person's life are deciding on a career and finding a job. This is not limited to recent college and university graduates but also to secondary school students contemplating future goals, to those of all ages perhaps relocating or changing careers and jobs, and to those seeking advancement into managerial positions.

Resources needed to pursue careers and job hunting include guides to occupations and outlooks for employment opportunities, résumés and cover letters, and preparation for the job interview.

The expansion of online job hunting resources has added to the dimension of materials available for deciding on a career and the job search itself.

ENCYCLOPEDIA

Encyclopedia of Careers and Vocational Guidance. 14th ed. New York: Ferguson, an imprint of InfoBase Publishing, 2008. 5 volumes.
  Contains entries for 93 career fields. Each career entry includes background of field/industry, structure, outlook, education/training required, words to know (jargon used), and resources for more information. Also provides guidance on how to find a job and interviewing.

GUIDES TO CAREERS AND JOB HUNTING

The following include guides to interviewing techniques, the résumé, and cover letters and to locating information about careers and occupations.

Adams Cover Letter Almanac. 2nd ed. Avon, MA, Adams Media, 2006.

Features sample cover letters, job hunting advice, the best and worst ways to find jobs, and cover letters by specific occupations (e.g., graphic artist). Contains approximately 600 sample cover letters.

Beshara, Tony. *Acing the Interview: How to Ask and Answer the Questions That Will Get You the Job.* New York: Amacom, 2008.

Beshara writes, "The emphasis in this book is not just to know how to answer and ask questions skillfully, but to put into context those answers and questions so that you not only can get a job offer, but choose the right one." Advises readers to understand their own context as well as that of the people they are interviewing with. The author has had 30 years of experience in the placement and recruitment field and is the owner of Babich and Associates.

Bolles, Richard N. *What Color Is Your Parachute: A Practical Manual for Job-Hunters and Career Changers.* Berkeley, CA: Ten Speed Press. Revised and updated annually.

This best-selling book's first edition was in 1972 and has been revised and updated every year since then. Bolles covers various aspects of finding a job and setting career goals, among which are the five best ways to look for a job, how to write a résumé, how to prepare for the job interview, salary negotiation, and how to choose a new career. Also included is the Flower Exercise, a series of questions enabling readers to determine the type of career where they can be happy, useful, and effective and also to evaluate strengths and weaknesses. Included is a sampler list of coaches or counselors and mentors to help through the process of career choices and career growth and development. The author also maintains a website, JobHuntersBible.com (http://www.jobhuntersbible.com) as a supplement to his books. Via this website, the author provides advice on the résumé, information on using the Internet to find a job, and links to related selected sites.

Career Builder.com (http://www.careerbuilder.com).

Resource for those looking for jobs features a searchable database and a list of recently posted jobs and allows users to post their résumés. Also allows searching by occupation. Within each occupation entry, articles and videos are posted, as are recent job opportunities.

Career Cruising (http://www.careercruising.com).

Requires a subscription. Career Cruising is an interactive career resource designed for people of all ages. Allows accessing of occupation profiles with a job description, information on salary and working conditions, education requirements, and a sample career path. Also provides guidance on effective job search techniques.

Career Library (*EBSCOhost*) (http://www.ebscohost.com/public/career -library).

Consists of five major components: The Exploration Center contains interest and skills assessment and search options for topics including occupation search, college search, financial aid information, apprenticeships, military occupations, college majors, state-specific data, occupation, and a video library. The Planning Center includes a résumé builder and college and career planning checklists. The Resource Center provides information on items including "cool jobs" (job profiles on up-and-coming or out-of-the -ordinary careers), Web resources, full-text articles, occupation video library, and state-specific data. The Help Center provides technical support with help files and frequently asked questions. The Activity Center is a testing center that enables users to take interactive quizzes on history and vocabulary, online polls, and so on.

Career Women (http://www.careerwomen.com).
   The site's goal is "helping women achieve success in their careers and lives" (website). A source of job postings allowing users to post their résumés. Features selected company profiles and searchable database of jobs (by key word, industry, state, and job category).

College Recruiter (http://collegerecruiter.com).
   For college students seeking internships and for recent college graduates looking for entry-level jobs. Also features an online résumé builder.

Compensation and Working Conditions (U.S. Bureau of Labor Statistics) (http://www.bls.gov/opub/cwc).
   Statistics on wages, health care, workplace safety, and so on. Provides salary information statistics for various occupations and includes results of selected job satisfaction surveys by occupations.

Criscito, Pat. *Resumes That Pop! Designs That Reflect Your Personal Brand.* 4th ed. Hauppauge, NY: Barron's Educational Series, 2010.
   Guide to preparing résumés that reflect the uniqueness of their authors: strengths, background, training, and career goals. Provides examples of types of résumés: functional, chronological, executive, curriculum vitae, and creative. Features 200 sample resumes and guide to creating and using electronic versions of the resume.

Dun & Bradstreet. *The Career Guide: The Employment Opportunities Directory.* Short Hills, NJ: Dun & Bradstreet. Annual.
   Directory of prospective employers and career opportunities. Entries are listed alphabetically, geographically, by industry classification, and by disciplines hired. Each entry includes name, address, telephone, Web address, percent range of white-collar employees, percent range of blue-collar employees, Standard Industrial Classification, occupations hired, and contacts.

Exploring Career Information from the Bureau of Labor Statistics (http://www.bls.gov/k12/index.htm).
   Online guide designed for students in grades 4 through 8 (teacher's guide is also provided) who are contemplating future careers. Researchers can select from several general career categories: reading, law, building and fixing things, math, science, music and arts, sports, helping people, managing money, nature, social studies, and computers. The category "Helping People" includes guides to occupations: teacher, child care

worker, firefighter, nurse, social worker, and doctor. For social worker, analysis is provided about what the job is like, the three major types of social work, educational requirements, future outlook, salary considerations, and statistics on number of jobs available. Cross-references to related occupations and further information are provided.

Job Agencies.com (http://jobagencies.com).
Directory of job agencies worldwide. Contains latest agencies and jobs and listings of agencies by industry and allows searching by key word.

Job Hunters Sourcebook: Where to Find Employment Leads and Other Job Search Resources. A Gale Career Information Guide. Kristy Harper, Project Editor. 10th ed. Farmington Hills, MI: Gale Cengage Learning, 2010. 3 volumes.
According to its introduction, the sourcebook is "a comprehensive guide to sources of information on employment leads and other job search resources." Provides advice on how to conduct the job search and contains listings of resources for job searchers. Contains three volumes. Volumes 1 and 2 contain sources of job hunting information listed by professions and occupations and identifies information sources for approximately 238 types of jobs. Materials identified include handbooks and manuals, online job sources and services, trade shows, and employee directories and networking lists. Volume 3 identifies sources of job hunting information that cover topics such as the job interview, opportunities for temporary workers, and electronic job search resources.

Job Web (http://www.jobweb.com).
A service of the National Association of Colleges and Employers. Provides guides to the job search, including sample résumés.

Krannich, Ronald L., and William J. Banis. *High Impact Resumes and Letters: How to Communicate Your Qualifications to Employers.* 9th ed. Manassas Park, VA: Impact Publications, 2006.
Guide to writing résumés and cover letters. Features sample résumés, cover letters, and thank-you résumés. Advises on mistakes not to make in a job search.

Kursmark, Louise M. *Best Resumes for College Students and New Grads: Jump-Start Your Career!* 2nd ed. St. Paul, MN: Jist Publishing, 2006.
For both undergraduate and graduate students, guide to writing résumés for the first job and also for internships and co-op jobs for those still in college.

Kursmark, Louise M., and Wendy S. Enelow. *Cover Letter Magic.* 4th ed. St. Paul, MN: Jist Publishing, 2010.
Guide on how to write the cover letter with advice from professional résumé and cover letter writers.

Monster.com (http://www.monster.com).
A major resource for finding jobs (allows users to post résumés and search for a job by title, skills, and location). Provides a guide to various aspects involved in the job search, résumé and cover letter writing, and

interviewing advice. Also provides an extensive guide to jobs and occupations, including career benchmarking (comparing salaries and locating jobs that are green, among other categories). Searchable database allows researchers to locate specific careers; the "Career Snapshots" section features a description of the occupation, required education/training, a list of currently available jobs, skills required (e.g., research skills), and industry/occupation forecast data.

The National Job Bank, by the Editors of Adams Media. Cincinnati: Adams Media. Annual. Print and CD. Option to purchase in print with CD or only on CD.

Features company profiles of over 20,000 employers. Section 1 consists of employer listings by state. Section 2 discusses conducting your job search. Section 3 is an index of companies by industry. Entries for each prospective employer include name, address, phone and fax numbers, contact person, number of employees, email and Web addresses, internship information, and so on.

Occupational Outlook Handbook (http://www.bls.gov/oco).

Revised every other year by the U.S. Department of Labor, Bureau of Labor Statistics. Available in hardcover, paper cover, and digital formats. The handbook is an essential source of career information, designed to assist individuals in choosing a career. This online edition enables researchers to browse specific occupations and also to search for specific jobs/occupations using the search box. To browse, searchers can select from major categories: management, professional, service, sales, administrative, farming, construction, installation, production, transportation, and armed forces. If a researcher, for example, chooses "Management," this selection will yield a list of more specific occupations, among which are education administrators, lodging managers, top executives, and loan officers. If the researcher selects "Lodging Managers," this entry will provide description of the nature of the work, training and qualifications, employment opportunities, job outlook, projections data, and median annual wages. Researchers are then referred to links to related occupations, such as food service managers, and also resources for further research (including websites of trade associations). The handbook also contains a "Special Features" section, providing links to career resources, financial aid information, education and training resources, and practical advice on the job search.

Plunkett, Jack. *The Almanac of American Employers.* Houston: Plunkett Research Ltd. Annual. Print and CD-ROM database.

Features analyses of major trends affecting the job seeker (employment). Lists 500 employers plus key associations and organizations of assistance to job seekers. Each entry in the 500 employers contains name, address, type of business, Web address, email, growth plans, financials, divisions, affiliates, salary information, locations, and contacts. Indexes by brand names and subsidiaries and an index of "Hot Spots for Advancement of Women and Minorities." Plunkett Research Ltd also publishes guides by industries for those searching for a focus on a specialized career (e.g., banking or telecommunications).

Quintessential Careers (http://www.quintcareers.com).
Contains a wide array of career resources and guides, including career assessment tools and tests, using a SWOT analysis in your career planning, career profiles, job hunting tools, writing résumés and cover letters, and links to job openings. The site is intended for job seekers, from teens to those seeking part-time jobs to those switching careers.

Salary.com (http://www.salary.com).
Search for salary information by job title and location.

Simply Hired (http://www.simplyhired.com).
Search for jobs by category and location or browse job categories. Also features searches by occupation for salaries and employment trends and by location (city and state) for employment and job trends (e.g., highest job growth or lowest unemployment rate).

Standard Occupational Classification (2010) (http://www.bls.gov/soc).
The *Standard Occupational Classification* (SOC) system "is used by Federal statistical agencies to classify workers into occupational categories for the purpose of collecting, calculating, or disseminating data. All workers are classified into one of 840 detailed occupations according to their occupational definition. To facilitate classification, detailed occupations are combined to form 461 broad occupations, 97 minor groups, and 23 major groups. Detailed occupations in the SOC with similar job duties, and in some cases skills, education, and/or training, are grouped together" (website). The 23 major groups are the following:

11-0000 Management Occupations
13-0000 Business and Financial Operations Occupations
15-0000 Computer and Mathematical Occupations
17-0000 Architecture and Engineering Occupations
19-0000 Life, Physical, and Social Science Occupations
21-0000 Community and Social Services Occupations
23-0000 Legal Occupations
25-0000 Education, Training, and Library Occupations
27-0000 Arts, Design, Entertainment, Sports, and Media Occupations
29-0000 Healthcare Practitioners and Technical Occupations
31-0000 Healthcare Support Occupations
33-0000 Protective Service Occupations
35-0000 Food Preparation and Serving Related Occupations
37-0000 Building and Grounds Cleaning and Maintenance Occupations
39-0000 Personal Care and Service Occupations
41-0000 Sales and Related Occupations
43-0000 Office and Administrative Support Occupations
45-0000 Farming, Fishing, and Forestry Occupations
47-0000 Construction and Extraction Occupations
49-0000 Installation, Maintenance, and Repair Occupations

51-0000 Production Occupations
53-0000 Transportation and Material Moving Occupations
55-0000 Military Specific Occupations

The 2010 edition is the most current-, and plans will be under way in 2013 for the 2018 SOC edition. The complete classification system is downloadable on the Bureau of Labor Statistics SOC website. SOC is searchable and browsable by name of occupation and also searchable by SOC number. An example of an SOC occupation entry is as follows:

25-1042 Biological Science Teachers, Postsecondary

Teach courses in biological sciences. Includes both teachers primarily engaged in teaching and those who do a combination of teaching and research.
Illustrative examples: *Botany Professor, Biochemistry Professor, Bacteriology Professor*

Broad Occupation: 25-1040 Life Sciences Teachers, Postsecondary
Minor Group: 25-1000 Postsecondary Teachers
Major Group: 25-0000 Education, Training, and Library Occupations

---

Vault Career Intelligence (http://www.vault.com/wps/portal/usa).
Offers fee-based résumé and cover letter services ("makeovers") and fee-based career coaching services. Also publishes a series of guides on careers and job hunting. Among its publications are *Vault Guide to the Top 50 Management and Strategy Consulting Firms* by Naomi Newman and guides to job opportunities, including *Vault Guide to the Top 50 Banking Employers* by Derek Loosvelt, *Vault Guide to the Top 25 Investment Management Employers* by Derek Loosvelt, *Vault Guide to Education Careers* by Jennifer Baker, and *Vault Career Guide to Advertising* by Ira Berkowitz.

Wall Street Journal: Careers (http://online.wsj.com/public/page/news-career-jobs.html).
Contains articles on career strategies, columns, and information about job search strategies.

OTHER RESOURCES

The On-Campus Career Center is a key source for undergraduate and graduate students looking for advice on the job search and their career options.

Additionally, public libraries feature resources for those seeking employment and investigating occupations. An example of this is the New York Public Library's Job Search Central@ SIBL (http://www.nypl.org/locations/tid/65/node/40820), a "one-stop shop" for job seekers featuring classes and programs and websites that list the latest jobs and provide advice on the job search.

Also, job expos and job fairs allow job seekers to meet prospective employers. Among the major job expos and job fairs are the following:

Career Builder.com Career Fairs (http://www.careerbuilder.com/JobSeeker/
    CareerFairs/default.aspx)
Job EXPO.com (http://www.jobexpo.com)
Job-Hunt.org (http://www.job-hunt.org/fairs.shtml)
National Career Fairs (http://www.nationalcareerfairs.com)

REGULATORY CONSIDERATIONS—PROHIBITED EMPLOYMENT POLICIES/HIRING PRACTICES

U.S. Equal Employment Opportunity Commission (http://www.eeoc.gov/
    laws/practices/index.cfm)
Focuses on fair hiring practice regulations.

PERIODICAL INDEXES AND FULL-TEXT DATABASES

Job seekers can research prospective employers and specific careers and industries using online databases: *ABI/INFORM* and *Business Source Premier*. Online regional newspaper databases (e.g., the *New York Times*) are also recommended for job and career research.

PERIODICALS

Career Development Quarterly (http://associationdatabase.com/aws/NCDA/
    pt/sp/cdquarterly)
Fast Company (http://www.fastcompany.com)
Insight into Diversity (http://www.insightintodiversity.com)
International Journal for Educational and Vocational Guidance (http://www
    .springerlink.com/content/106602)
Journal of Career Assessment (http://jca.sagepub.com)
Journal of Career Development (http://jcd.sagepub.com)
Occupational Outlook Quarterly (http://www.bls.gov/opub/ooq/home.htm)
Wall Street Journal (http://online.wsj.com/home-page)
Work and Occupations (http://wox.sagepub.com)
Working Mother Magazine (http://www.workingmother.com/?service
    =vpage/106)

14

Accounting

Accounting is defined as the "process of reporting, measuring, interpreting, and communicating financial data" (*Dictionary of Accounting Terms*). The earliest accounting records, which date back approximately 7,000 years, were found in the ruins of ancient Babylon, Assyria, and Sumeria. Bookkeeping, using clay tables, was done to measure the growth of crops and livestock. Subsequently, more sophisticated accounting records were found in examining historical documents of the Roman Empire and medieval Europe, and the person referred to the father of accounting, Luca Pacioli (1446–1517), wrote the first known treatise on bookkeeping.

Accounting today is comprised of various branches with various job specializations available. Financial accounting involves recording business transactions and preparation of financial statements, including the balance sheet and income statement and recording any changes n financial position. These statements are staples of a company's annual report, and this information is distributed to investors, potential investors, or anyone interested in researching the company. Financial accounting information must conform with generally accepted accounting principles (GAAP). Management or managerial accounting is the analysis, preparation, measurement, interpretation, and communication of financial data used within a company by management for evaluation and planning purposes. Auditing is an examination of a client's (including companies and nonprofit agencies) financial records by an independent certified public accountant (CPA). Auditing procedures must conform with generally accepted auditing procedures. Taxation (see Chapter 14) is the charge by a government (e.g., federal or state) on individuals, corporations, and so on, with the funds collected used for projects and programs related to the public good.

Research materials for accounting practitioners and students include encyclopedias and dictionaries, the standards of various agencies and associations, directories, handbooks, test preparation for CPA exams, journal articles, and resources related to international accounting practices.

ENCYCLOPEDIAS AND DICTIONARIES

The Blackwell Encyclopedic Dictionary of Accounting. Edited by A. Rashad Abdel-Khalik. Malden, MA: Blackwell, 1998.

> With entries primarily by university faculty, this source is arranged in alphabetical order, with index, cross-references and bibliographical references. Among the entries are those for accounting for leases standards, capital budgeting, earnings per share, statistical sampling in auditing, and income classification and reporting.

The History of Accounting: An International Encyclopedia. Edited by Michael Chatfield and Richard Vangermeersch. New York: Garland Publishing, 1996.

> Focuses on the history of accounting and accounting thought. Entries include names of historically influential individuals, court cases, terms, names of countries, and names of agencies. Cross-references are included, as are an index and bibliographical references. Alphabetically arranged topics include ledger, law and accounting, Charles Babbage, balance sheet, Securities and Exchange Commission, and uniform accounting.

Law, Jonathan. *A Dictionary of Accounting.* 4th ed. New York: Oxford University Press, 2010.

> Provides over 3,600 entries related to accounting with cross-references and an appendix of useful websites. For abbreviations, entries list full name with cross-references for selected entries. Among the terms defined are average cost, audit, machine hour, budget period, and discussion memorandum.

Siegel, Joel G., and Jae K. Shim. *Dictionary of Accounting Terms.* 5th ed. Hauppauge, NY: Barron's Educational Series, Inc., 2010.

> Covers approximately 2,500 accounting-related terms. Includes cross-references. Definitions include audit guide, accounting cushion, classification of assets, productivity measures, managerial/management accounting, and financial accounting and entries for agencies including the American Accounting Association and the American Institute of Certified Public Accountants. Appendices contain acronyms and abbreviations and tables (e.g., "Present Value of $1.00").

DIRECTORIES

Who Audits America: A Directory of Publicly Traded Companies and the Accounting Firms Who Audit Them. Menlo Park, CA: Data Financial Press. Semiannual. Database also available for rental in Excel format.

This directory is organized as follows: part A: "Master Company List," contains entries for companies and identifies auditor and former auditor (where applicable, ticker symbol, number of employees, and financials); part B: :Auditors, Auditor Summary," lists auditors, listing total number of clients; part C: "The 'Big-4' Accounting Firms' U.S. Audit Clients, Sales of 1 Billion Plus"; part D: "The Non 'Big-4' Accounting Firms—All U.S. Clients of All Non-Big 4 Auditors; and part E: "The State Lists, All Clients of All Auditors, Nationwide—Listed by State." Appendices include auditor list by codes and Standard Industrial Classification and state codes.

Yahoo! Directory: Accounting Firms (http://dir.yahoo.com/business_and _economy/business_to_business/financial_services/accounting/firms). Directory. Includes links to websites of accounting firms.

HANDBOOK

Carmichael, D. R., and Paul H. Rosenfield. *Accountants' Handbook.* 11th ed. New York: Wiley, 2007. 2 volumes. Also available as an ebook through NetLibrary.

The stated goal in the preface is to "provide in a single reference source answers to all reasonable questions on accounting that might be asked by accountants, auditors, executives, bankers, lawyers, financial analysts, and other preparers and users of financial information." Volume 1, "Financial Accounting and General Topics," is a review of the framework of accounting and general aspects of financial statement presentation. Specific topics, written by experts in the field, include SEC reporting requirements, financial statements form and content, the framework of financial accounting concepts and standards, inventory, leases, liabilities, and auditing standards and audit reports. Volume 2, "Special Industries and Special Topics," focuses on the specialized environment and accounting considerations for specific industries and accounting standards applying to retirement and pension plans as well as on topics related to partnership, estates, and trusts. Specific topics covered in volume include bankruptcy, not-for-profit organizations, providers of health care services, accounting for government contracts, and valuation of nonpublic companies. Contains sample statements, and each article contains sources and suggested references for further research.

ACCOUNTING STANDARDS

Accounting standards are available in both digital and print formats.

Accounting Research Manager (CCH, a Wolters Kluwer Business) (http://
www.accountingresearchmanager.com/ARMMenu.nsf/vwHTML/
ARMSplash?OpenDocument).
   Browse or search the full text of accounting standards. Contents to this
   extensive database include accounting standards of AICIPA, FASB,
   BTF (Business Tax Forum), and IASB (International Accounting
   Standards Board); government accounting standards of the General
   Accountability Office, GASB (Governmental Accounting Standards
   Board), and OMB (Office of Management and Budget); and auditing
   standards of OMB (Office of Management and Budget) and PCAOB.
   Also includes selected full-text material from the Securities and
   Exchange Commission.

American Institute of Certified Public Accountants. *Statements on Auditing
   Standards.* New York: AICPA. Loose-leaf service.
   For auditing standards, contains introduction, effective date, objective,
   requirements, and application.

Financial Accounting Research System FARS on CD-ROM. Financial Accounting
   Standards Board (http://www.fasb.org/fars).
   CD-ROM format can be installed on a personal computer in stand-alone or
   networked configuration, FARS contains the full text of *Original Pronouncements* (including FASB and AICPA pronouncements); *Original Pronouncements: As Amended, Including Implementation Guides and FASB Staff
   Positions; ETF Abstracts* (includes full-text abstracts of every issue discussed
   by the Emerging Issues Task Force since 1984); *Comprehensive Topical Index;
   and Derivatives Codification.*

Financial Accounting Standards Board. *Current Text.* Norwalk, CT: Financial
   Accounting Standards Board. Annual. 2 volumes.
   An integration of the financial accounting and reporting standards
   included in the *Original Pronouncements as Amended,* arranged by topic
   for general and industry standards.

Financial Accounting Standards Board (https://www.fasb.org/store). Free
   downloadable PDF documents.
   These documents contain full texts of FASB accounting standards updates,
   concepts statements, and precodification standards.

Financial Accounting Standards Board. *Exposure Documents Available for
   Comment* (http://www.fasb.org/jsp/FASB/Page/SectionPage&cid
   =1175801893139).
   Contains text of exposure drafts (proposed standards) and discussion
   papers (used to solicit input on major issues addressed in a project.

Financial Accounting Standards Board. *Original Pronouncements as Amended.*
   Norwalk, CT: Financial Accounting Standards Board. Annual. 3 volumes
   Contains all pronouncements in an "as amended" format, including FASB
   statements of standards, concepts statements, interpretations, technical

bulletins; FASB staff positions; and AICPA APB opinions, interpretations, and accounting research bulletins.

GAAP Guide. Chicago: CCH, a Wolters Kluwer Business. Annual.
Contains Volume 1, *Restatement and Analysis of Current FASB Standards*, and volume 2, *Restatement and Analysis of Other Current FASB, EITF, and AICPA Pronouncements.*

Governmental Accounting Research System (GARS) (Governmental Accounting Standards Board.
CD-ROM format that contain the contents of all the annual bound GARS editions.

STANDARDS SETTING ORGANIZATIONS

American Institute of Certified Public Accountants (AICPA) (http://www.aicpa.org/Pages/Default.aspx).
Professional association for certified public accountants in the United States. Its stated purpose is to serve "the CPA profession and the public interest . . . AICPA members work in all sectors of the business and financial services profession (website). Establishes accounting and auditing standards.

Financial Accounting Standards Board (FASB) (http://www.fasb.org/home).
The mission of the FASB is "to establish and improve standards of financial accounting and reporting that foster financial reporting by nongovernmental entities that provides decision-useful information to investors and other users of financial reports" (website). Develops generally accepted accounting principles for the accounting profession.

Financial Accounting Standards Board. Emerging Issues Task Force (EITF) (http://www.fasb.org/jsp/FASB/Page/SectionPage&cid=1218220137512).
The mission of the EITF is "to assist the FASB in improving financial reporting through the timely identification, discussion, and resolution of financial accounting issues within the framework of the FASB Accounting Standards Codification™ (Accounting Standards Codification), which represents the source of authoritative standards of accounting and reporting, other than those issued by the SEC, to be applied by nongovernmental entities" (website).

Government Accounting Standards Board (GASB) (http://www.gasb.org).
GASB's stated mission is "to establish and improve standards of state and local governmental accounting and financial reporting that will: result in useful information for users of financial reports and guide and educate the public, including issuers, auditors, and users of those financial report . . . subject to oversight by the Financial Accounting Foundation's Board of Trustees" (website).

IFRS Foundation and the IASB. International Financial Reporting Standards and the International Accounting Standards Board (http://www.ifrs.org/Home.htm).

Issue the following standards: *International Financial Reporting Standards,* issued after 2001; *International Accounting Standards,* issued prior to 2001; and *Interpretations Originated* from the International Financial Reporting Interpretations Committee, issued after 2001.

INTERNATIONAL ACCOUNTING

Transnational Accounting. 2nd ed. Edited by Dieter Ordelheide and KPMG. Hampshire: Palgrave, 2001. 3 volumes.

Reference guide to important accounting systems in the world. Covers 19 countries plus the European Union and the International Accounting Standards Committee. Countries included are Argentina, Canada, the United States, Australia, Japan, Austria, Belgium, Denmark, Finland, France, Germany, Italy, the Netherlands, Portugal, Spain, Sweden, Norway, Switzerland, and the United Kingdom. Entries for each company analyze and describe financial reporting practices, forms of business organization, objectives of financial reporting, balance sheet, and recognition criteria and valuation.

FINANCIAL REPORTING PRACTICES

Accounting Trends & Techniques: Presenting and Analyzing Financial Reporting Practices. New York: AICPA. Annual.

This source "compiles annual reporting and disclosure data and examples from a survey of the annual reports of publicly traded companies" (preface). Contains hundreds of illustrative entries from prominent publicly traded companies in the United States, presenting the latest trends in presentation and disclosures. Appendix contains a list of 500 survey entities and where the text excerpts from their annual reports can be found, with pronouncement and subject indexes.

MAJOR ACCOUNTING ORGANIZATIONS AND WEBSITES

Academy of Accounting Historians (http://www.aahhq.org).

The stated objectives of the academy are "to encourage research, publication, teaching and personal interchanges in all phases of Accounting History and its interrelation with business and economic history" (website).

Accounting Web (http://www.accountingweb.com).

Provides accounting news, tips, tools, and resources for accountants.

American Accounting Association (http://aaahq.org).
  For academic audiences, this association promotes excellence in accounting education, research, and practice.

Association of Government Accountants (http://www.agacgfm.org/
  homepage.aspx).
  Supports the careers and professional development of government finance
  professionals working in federal, state and local governments as well as
  the private sector and academia" (website).

Institute of Internal Auditors (http://www.theiia.org).
  The internal auditor's "leader in certification, education, research, and
  technical guidance" (website).

Institute of Management Accountants (http://www.imanet.org/ima
  _home.aspx).
  Worldwide association for financial professionals and accountants working in business.

International Federation of Accountants (http://www.ifac.org).
  Global organization for the accounting profession.

WebCPA (http://www.webcpa.com).
  Provides latest news, resources, and tips for the certified public accountant.

PERIODICAL INDEXES AND FULL-TEXT DATABASES

In addition to consulting, *ABI/INFORM*, *Business Source Premier*,
ScienceDirect, *JSTOR*, and the *Wall Street Journal* (ProQuest) databases,
the following specialized searchable databases should be consulted by
researchers:

Accounting Research Network (http://www.ssrn.com/arn/index.html).
  Includes index to working papers in accounting.

Digital Accounting Collection. University of Mississippi (http://umiss.lib
  .olemiss.edu:82).
  Provides full-text access to back files of the *Accounting Historians Journal*,
  back files of the *Accounting Historians Notebook*, back files of AICPA's
  Exposure Drafts and *Codes of Professional Conduct*, and full-text accounting
  pamphlets.

LexisNexis Academic Universe (http://www.lexisnexis.com/hottopics/
  lnacademic/?).
  Select "Accounting" under "Subject Areas" to locate full-text access to
  accounting publications, including the following publications: *Accounting
  Today, Accounting Technology, AICPA Accounting and Auditing Publications,
  AICPA-CPA Letter (1988–1999), Controller Report, Journal of Accountancy,
  Practical Accountant, Accounting Series Releases, Accountant's Handbook,
  Accountant's Liability,* and *John Wiley Publications*.

ProQuest Accounting and Tax Index (http://www.proquest.com/en-US/
  catalogs/databases/detail/pq_accounting_tax.shtml).
  Indexes and abstracts, with some full-text coverage, and provides access to
  global and scholarly journals, including all journals from the American
  Accounting Association; tax management and auditing trade publications; AICPA publications; and over 1,500 accounting dissertations and
  selected working papers and conference proceedings. Also available in
  print format and published by AICPA.

MAJOR JOURNALS

Accountancy Age (http://www.accountancyage.com)
Accounting and Business Research (http://www.abr-journal.com)
Accounting, Auditing and Accountability Journal (http://www.emeraldinsight
  .com/products/journals/journals.htm)
Accounting Education: An International Journal (http://www.tandf.co.uk/
  journals/titles/09639284.asp)
Accounting Review (http://aaahq.org/pubs/acctrev.htm)
CPA Journal (http://www.cpajournal.com)
International Journal of Accounting (http://www.elsevier.com/wps/find/
  journaldescription.cws_home/620179/description#description)
Journal of Accountancy (http://www.journalofaccountancy.com)
Journal of Accounting Literature (http://warrington.ufl.edu/fsoa/faculty/
  jal.asp)
Journal of Accounting Research (http://www.wiley.com/bw/journal.asp?ref
  =0021-8456)
Journal of International Financial Management and Accounting (http://www
  .wiley.com/bw/journal.asp?ref=0954-1314)
Management Accounting Quarterly (http://www.imanet.org/resources_and
  _publications/management_accounting_quarterly.aspx)

CPA EXAMINATION GUIDES

Those who wish to become certified public accountants in the United
States are required to pass the Uniform CPA Examination. The CPA
Exam, delivered in computer-based format, measures skills in analy-
sis, judgment, communication, research, and understanding.

American Institute of Certified Public Accountants. *Guide to the CPA Examination*
  (http://www.aicpa.org/BecomeACPA/CPAExam/Pages/CPAExam.aspx).
  Guide to and description of the Uniform CPA Exam.

American Institute of Certified Public Accountants. *Uniform CPA Examination
  Alert* (http://www.cpa2biz.com/AST/Main/CPA2BIZ_Primary/
  PRDOVR~PC-EXAMALERT/PC-EXAMALERT.jsp).

Quarterly newsletter. Online publication contains information about changes to the Uniform CPA Examination.

Wiley CPA Exam Review, by O. Ray Whittington and Patrick L. Delaney. Hoboken, NJ: Wiley, Annual. 2 volumes.

Contains review of AICPA Content Specification Outlines for the Computerized CPA Examination, discussion of simulation-style questions, coverage of new accounting and auditing standards, and coverage of changes in the CPA examination. Volume 1 contains outlines and study guides, and volume 2 contains problems and solutions.

15

Taxation

Taxation is a part of life for the U.S. citizen and has developed and evolved over the past few centuries. After the Revolutionary War, under the Articles of Confederation (1781), each state was considered a sovereign entity and could levy tax if it so wished. In 1789, with the adoption of the Constitution, Congress was given the power to "lay and collect taxes, duties, imposts, and excises, pay the Debts and provide for the common Defense and general Welfare of the United States." To pay for the costs of a U.S. conflict with France in the late 1790s, the federal government imposed the first direct taxes (taxes on individuals who owned homes, estates, and land). Taxes were imposed to raise money for the War of 1812, including additional excise taxes, raising of some customers duties, and issuing of Treasury notes. In 1817, Congress repealed all internal taxes and relied and relied on tariffs on imported goods to raise funds for support of the government. For the next 44 years no internal revenue was collected by the federal government. This changed during the time of the Civil War.

THE INTERNAL REVENUE SERVICE AND TAX REGULATION

The concept of a central agency collecting taxes began during the Civil War in 1862. President Abraham Lincoln created a position of a commissioner of internal revenue and enacted an income tax to be collected to pay Civil War expenses. This income tax was repealed in 1872, and another income tax was enacted in 1894 but was declared unconstitutional by the Supreme Court in 1895.

In 1913, the Sixteenth Amendment gave Congress the authority to enact an income tax, and the first Form 1040 was created after Congress levied a 1 percent tax on net personal income above $3,000 and a 6 percent surtax on incomes over $500,000. Tax rates then varied in these earliest years: during World War I, the top income tax rate was 77 percent to pay for the war effort, then down to 24 percent in 1929, with an increase again during the Depression. The name of what is now known as the Internal Revenue Service (IRS) was the Bureau of Internal Revenue.

During the 1950s, there was a reorganization, and professional employees were utilized. The name of the agency became the IRS. Through the IRS Restructuring and Reform Act of 1998, a major reorganization took place, with the IRS reorganized to "closely resemble the private sector of organizing around customers with similar needs" (IRS website).

The IRS is a bureau of the U.S. Department of the Treasury. The current organization of the IRS is divided into three commissioner-level organizations: commissioner (units on this level report directly to the Commissioner's office), deputy commissioner for services and enforcement, and deputy commissioner for operations support.

The IRS Mission is to as follows

The IRS Mission

Provide America's taxpayers top quality service by helping them understand and meet their tax responsibilities and enforce the law with integrity and fairness to all.

This mission statement describes our role and the public's expectation about how we should perform that role.

- In the United States, the Congress passes tax laws and requires taxpayers to comply.
- The taxpayer's role is to understand and meet his or her tax obligations.
- The IRS role is to help the large majority of compliant taxpayers with the tax law, while ensuring that the minority who are unwilling to comply pay their fair share. (IRS website)

Internal Revenue Service (IRS) (http://www.irs.gov).

Contains a wide array of resources for taxpayers, among which are downloadable tax forms, electronic filing, taxpayer advocate service, instructions for filling out tax forms, information on taxpayer rights, frequently asked questions, links to agencies by state (e.g., taxation, employer, and small business links), news releases, and information for international taxpayers. This website is a staple source for anyone filing taxes, students researching information about taxes, and any related interest.

U.S. Department of the Treasury (http://www.ustreas.gov).
  This department describes collecting taxes in a fair and consistent manner as a core mission. The Department of the Treasury "enforces nation's tax laws fairly and efficiently while balancing taxpayer service and education to provide and promote voluntary compliance and reduce taxpayer burden" (website).

STATE AND LOCAL TAXES

State and local agencies provide websites for information about tax collections, including forms to be downloaded as well as guides. For example, the New York State Department of Taxation and Finance (http://www.tax.state.ny.us) provides access to forms, regulations, on-line payments, and recent tax law changes. The IRS website contains a directory of key state agencies, including those related to taxation (http://www.irs.gov/businesses/small/article/0,,id=99021,00.html). Search engines such as Google allow searching for specific state agencies.

TAX LAW AND CASES

The Internal Revenue Code is the basis of U.S. tax law and court cases related to tax involve interpretations of this code. The following section examines these specific sources and where to locate them with interpretations by commercial publishers.

The code is available through several government and commercial sources. Its link on the IRS site is as follows:

Internal Revenue Code of 1986 (http://www.irs.gov/taxpros/article/0,, id=98137,00.html).
  Federal tax law begins with the Internal Revenue Code. Court cases, regulations, revenue rulings, and revenue procedures "attempt to properly interpret the Internal Revenue Code. The code has been amended with each subsequent Tax Reform Act.

Internal Revenue Service. *Internal Revenue Bulletin* (http://www.irs.gov/irb).
  A resource for keeping track of documents related to tax law, including revenue rulings, revenue procedures, IRS notices, and news releases. Prior to their publication in the bulletin, the IRS issues an "Advanced Notice for Tax Professionals" (http://www.irs.gov/taxpros/article/0,, id=98697,00.html) in advance of their publication. These advanced notices, called "early drops" by the IRS, are available for retrieval.

INTERPRETATIONS OF THE INTERNAL REVENUE CODE THROUGH COURT CASES:

The U.S. Tax Court (http://www.ustaxcourt.gov).
   The Tax Court is described as the "court of record established by Congress under Article I of the U.S. Constitution. When the Commissioner of Internal Revenue has determined a tax deficiency, the taxpayer may dispute the deficiency in the Tax Court before paying any disputed amount. The Tax Court's jurisdiction also includes the authority to redetermine transferee liability, make certain types of declaratory judgments, adjust partnership items, order abatement of interest, award administrative and litigation costs, redetermine worker classification, determine relief from joint and several liability on a joint return, review certain collection actions, and review awards to whistleblowers who provide information to the Commissioner of Internal Revenue on or after December 20, 2006" (website). Decisions of the Tax Court are in two categories: U.S. Tax Court regular opinions (officially published opinions) and U.S. Tax Court memo decisions (which are not published officially or designated as a "regular" opinion).

SOURCES CONTAINING TAX LAW AND CASES

Commerce Clearing House *CCH Tax Research Network* (http://www.cch.com).
   Online database contents include full texts of tax codes, Federal tax cases, state tax cases, treaties, regulations, rulings, IRS publications, and CCH interpretations and analysis.

Daily Tax Report. BNA Tax and Accounting (http://www.bnatax.com/Daily-Tax-Report-p7889). Print and online.
   Source for news on key federal, state, and international legislative, regulatory, and judicial tax-related developments. Contains full text of key documents and analysis by BNA editors. Also available with real-time summaries emailed to subscribers and TaxCores, a database of full-text searchable documents from Congress and the IRS, among other sources.

LexisNexis Academic Universe. U.S. Tax Law (http://www.lexisnexis.com/hot-topics/lnacademic/?).
   Tax Law is a searchable database to full-text coverage of publications: Internal Revenue Code; Treasury regulations; attorney general tax opinions, federal and state tax cases; law review tax articles; IRS bulletins, rulings, and decisions; tax analysts publications; and *The Tax Lawyer, The Practical Tax Lawyer,* and *The Tax Advisor.*

RIA Checkpoint (Thomson Reuters) (http://ria.thomsonreuters.com/Tax Research/taxation.asp).
   Full-text access to the Internal Revenue Code, the *RIA Federal Tax Handbook,* federal tax regulations, and court cases.

Shepard's Federal Tax Citation (*LexisNexis*) (http://www.lexisnexis.com/store/ catalog/booktemplate/productdetail.jsp;jsessionid=F45912724B4E 948FF9BC4D787F42EB13.psc1705_lnstore_001?pageName=relatedProducts &catId=121&prodId=10990).

Searchable database. Gathers cases and citations of cases. Sources are *Shepardized* to validate their authorities.

U.S. Master Tax Guide. Chicago: Commerce Clearing House, a Wolters Kluwer business. Annual.

Provides explanation of federal income taxes for individuals, partnerships, corporations, estates and trusts, and new rules established by key court decisions and the IRS.

TAX STATISTICS

Internal Revenue Service. Statistics (http://www.irs.gov/taxstats/index.html). Among statistics provided are number of individual returns filed by county, charitable and exempt organization statistics, statistics by form, and business statistics. The "Tax Statistics at a Glance" section lists the total number of returns for individuals and corporations, estate taxes, gift taxes, employment taxes, and excise taxes.

Westlaw Tax (http://west.thomson.com/westlaw/westlaw-tax/default.aspx). Searchable full-text database contains access to federal and state sources on tax law (statutes, regulations, and cases), IRS publications and other federal and state agency materials, and analytical resources from publishers such as BNA, West, and WG & L.

ENCYCLOPEDIAS AND DICTIONARIES

The following sources provide definitions of tax terms and, in the case of the encyclopedia on tax policy, provide in-depth articles on the various aspects of taxation.

Crumbley, D. Larry, Jack P. Friedman, and Susan B. Anders. *Dictionary of Tax Terms.* Hauppauge, NY: Barron's Educational Series, 1994.

Defines tax-related terms, among which are information return, Internal Revenue Service, Revenue Ruling (Rev. Rul.), capital loss, and gift tax.

The Encyclopedia of Taxation and Tax Policy. Edited by Joseph J. Cordes, Robert D. Ebel, and Jane G. Gravelle. 2nd ed. Baltimore: Urban Institute Press, 2005.

Coverage of federal, state, local, and international tax policy issues; types of taxes (individual, corporate, estate, property, and so on); and legislation. Contributors of essays are academics, tax practitioners and administrators, and policymakers. Includes bibliographical references for further research.

Law, Jonathan. *A Dictionary of Accounting*. 4th ed. New York: Oxford University Press, 2010.
Contains definitions related to taxation, among which are tax credit, tax deductible, tax relief, tax tables, and Internal Revenue Code.

Siegel, Joel G., and Jae K. Shim. *Dictionary of Accounting Terms*. 5th ed. Hauppauge, NY: Barron's Educational Series, 2010.
Coverage includes definitions of tax terms, among which are names of major laws and agencies. Among the terms defined are tax, Internal Revenue Service, tax haven, tax evasion, tax rate, and the Tax Act of 1993.

Westin, Richard A. W G and L Tax Dictionary. Boston: Warren, Gorham and Lamont, 2007.
Contains approximately 4000 definitions of terms, including slang, agencies, and legislation.

MAJOR WEBSITES

American Taxation Association (http://aaahq.org/ATA/index.htm).
Founded in 1974, features news reports, announcements of meetings, and access to back files of periodicals: *ATA Newsletter* and access for members only to the *Journal of the American Tax Association* and the *Journal of Legal Tax Research*.

Bankrate.com: Taxes (http://www.bankrate.com/taxes.aspx).
Features include tax calculators, taxes blog, rate watch, news reports, and tax advice.

MSN Money Central: Tax (http://articles.moneycentral.msn.com/taxes/home.aspx).
Contains tax news, tax tips, advice on how to avoid an audit, a glossary, and tax calendars, among other features.

National Association of Tax Professionals (http://www.natptax.com/Pages/default.aspx).
For tax professionals "providing the support, education, products, and services they need to succeed in the tax profession" (website). Contains press releases and offers publications for sale, among which are the periodical *TAXPRO Weekly*.

National Tax Association (NTA) (http://ntanet.org).
The NTA "brings together a unique membership of government, corporate, academic, and independent tax professionals; a rich mix of scholars; federal, state, and local legislators and administrators; taxpayer representatives; tax lawyers and accountants; professors and other scholars; students and interested citizens" (website). Provides a forum for debate and research. Publisher of the *National Tax Journal*, contains links to relevant websites and provides news of their conferences.

Tax History Project (Tax Analysts) (http://www.taxhistory.org).
  Designed for researchers or anyone interested in the history of U.S. public finance. Contains article archive, images, a chronology of tax history, images of tax returns over the years, and records of presidential tax returns.

TaxSites.com (http://www.taxsites.com).
  List of links to a variety of sites, among which are associations, guides, tax software, rates and tables, IRS links, and tax tips.

Yahoo! Finance—Taxes (http://finance.yahoo.com/taxes).
  Contains current news items, a series of how-to guides on various tax topics, calculators, and expert opinions.

DATABASES AND PERIODICAL INDEXES

In addition to accessing the major business online databases—*Business Source Premier, ABI/INFORM, JSTOR*, and, for scholarly articles, *ScienceDirect*—two specialized sources for taxation include the following:

Index to Federal Tax Articles. New York: Thomson Reuters.
  Index to periodical articles on federal tax, estate tax, or gift tax. Articles indexed are from legal journals, specialized tax journals, economic journals, and tax institutes. Multivolume set: Volumes 1 and 2 list major articles from 1913 to mid-1974, indexed by topic. Volume 3 lists entries from 1913 to mid-1974 by author names. Cumulative volumes cover 1974–1981, 1982–1983, 1984–1987, 1989–1992, 1993–1996, and 1997–2004; there is also a cumulative volume for 2005 and a user's guide volume.

ProQuest Accounting and Tax Database
  (http://www.proquest.com/en-US/catalogs/databases/detail/pq _accounting_tax.shtml).

  Contains full-text coverage of topics related to tax management and tax law (from sources including the American Bar Association and the American law Institute).

MAJOR JOURNALS

International Tax Review (http://www.internationaltaxreview.com)
Journal of International Taxation (http://ria.thomsonreuters.com/estore/ detail.aspx?ID=WJIT&SITE=/taxresearch/international)
Journal of Taxation (http://ria.thomsonreuters.com/estore/detail.aspx?ID =JTAX)
The Kiplinger Tax Letter (https://www.kiplinger.com/orders/ktl2)
National Tax Journal (http://ntj.tax.org)

Tax Features (http://www.taxfoundation.org/publications/showtype/
    26.html)
TAXES—The Tax Magazine (http://onlinestore.cch.com/productdetail.asp
    ?productid=591)

TAX PREPARATION GUIDES

During tax season, public libraries particularly need to stock up on
guides to filing taxes. These guides offer step-by-step advice on how
to file income taxes—updated each year to reflect changes in forms
and tax schedules. It should also be remembered that the IRS website
contains resource material designed for those preparing their taxes.
For state and local, the websites for these agencies can be consulted.

Some recommended titles on how to prepare taxes are the following:

Botkin, Sandy. *Lower Your Taxes—Big Time!* New York: McGraw-Hill. Annual.
J. K. Lasser's Your Income Tax. Hoboken, NJ: Wiley. Annual.
Schnepper, Jeff. *How to Pay Zero Taxes.* New York: McGraw-Hill. Annual.
Tax for Dummies. Hoboken, NJ: Wiley. Annual.
Weltman, Barbara. *J. K. Lasser's 1001 Deductions and Tax Breaks.* Hoboken, NJ:
    Wiley. Annual.

16

Real Estate

Buying a home is a major event in anyone's life, and potential home owners need to examine such key issues as whether to rent or buy, finding the best rates for a mortgage, and maintaining the home. Other key decisions can be selling a home, investing in property and homes, and becoming a landlord. Questions related to real estate include finding the basics and finding practical guides, locating databases to search for a home and mortgage rates, finding property and real estate for investment purposes, and, for researchers, needing statistics on, for example, housing starts, home prices, and numbers of homes sold per year.

Types of real estate are residential (private houses, apartments, co-ops, and condominiums), commercial (stores, shopping centers, office buildings, hotels, motels, and restaurants) and industrial (factories and warehouses).

This chapter describes the major resources for anyone interested in buying and selling a home and providing information and data to make the right decisions plus researching the market.

ENCYCLOPEDIAS AND DICTIONARIES

Abbott, Damien. *Encyclopedia of Real Estate Terms*. 3rd ed. London: Delta Alpha Publishing, 2008.
International in scope, this encyclopedia provides definitions for approximately 10,000 terms and provides cross-references and citations of relevant court cases provided with entries (where applicable). Features a bibliography, a summary of major real estate laws, a list of international professional associations, and real estate acronyms and abbreviations.

Friedman, Jack P., Jack C. Harris, and J. Bruce Lindeman. *Dictionary of Real Estate Terms*. 7th ed. Hauppauge, NY: Barron's Educational Series, 2008.
Provides definitions of approximately 3,000 real estate–related terms, with cross-references and a list of acronyms and abbreviations plus line drawings and charts with selected definitions. Covers mortgages, construction, appraisal, zoning, and so on.

Haden, Jeff. *The Complete Dictionary of Real Estate Terms: Explained Simply: What Smart Investors Need to Know*. Ocala, FL: Atlantic Publishing, 2007.
Covers over 2,400 definitions of terms and jargon used in real estate among, which are abstract of title, escheat, recital, open house, and commission.

Holton, Lisa. *The Essential Dictionary of Real Estate: Completely Up-to-Date; Over 3,000 Real Estate Terms Explained*. New York: Barnes & Noble, 2004.
Provides definitions for approximately 2,000 terms and contains charts, graphs, and illustrations for selected definitions.

GUIDES

Crook, David. *The Wall Street Journal Complete Home Owner's Guidebook: Making the Most of Your Biggest Asset on Any Market*. New York: Three Rivers Press, 2008.
Practical guide to buying and owning a home. Covers the topics of buying versus renting, advice for first-time home owners, maintaining a home, how to make the best profit on selling, and trading up.

Crook, David. *The Wall Street Journal Complete Real Estate Investing Guidebook*. New York: Three Rivers Press, 2006.
A look at real estate as an investment. Provides practical advice on various topics, among which are financing concerns, how to select and buy property, mortgages, issues involved in becoming a landlord, and how to sell a property and trade up.

Friedman, Jack P., Jack C. Harris, and Barry A. Diskin. *Barron's Real Estate Handbook*. 7th ed. Hauppauge, NY: Barron's Educational Series, 2009.
Guide designed for home buyers and sellers, investors, real estate agents, and those considering a career in real estate. Provides a home buyer's guide, financing options, investing in real estate, careers in real estate, regulatory issues, and a glossary and guide to information sources. Features housing market data, sample forms, and monthly mortgage payment figures calculated across a range of annual interest rates.

Reed, David. *Mortgages 101: Quick Answers to Over 250 Critical Questions about Your Home Loan*. 2nd ed. New York: AMACOM, 2008.
Written in question-and-answer format, this practical guide covers various topics of interest to those buying a home and seeking mortgages. These topics include the difference between buying and renting, what a down payment is, finding the best lender, refinancing, closing costs, and finding the best interest rates. Features a glossary of terms.

Yahoo! Finance—Real Estate (http://finance.yahoo.com/real-estate).
 Features online how-to guides, including "Buying Your First Home,"
 "Remodeling Your Home," and "Your Home and Your Retirement." Also
 contains calculators on mortgage calculation, refinancing, and renting
 versus owning and question and answers from experts in real estate, a
 searchable database of homes for sale, and current lending rates.

DATA AND STATISTICS SOURCES

Company information about real estate companies and related companies such as construction firms may be researched through the databases Dun & Bradstreet, Mergent, Standard & Poor's, and Hoover's.

The following resources contain data about new homes for sale,
mortgage data, foreclosures, housing starts, and industry data related
to the real estate, construction, and housing markets.

Bloomberg: Real Estate (http://www.bloomberg.com/news/real-estate).
 Source of information on the latest real estate news releases, including
 articles on home values and mortgage rates. Tracks the latest data.

CNN Money.com Real Estate (http://money.cnn.com/real_estate).
 Features news stories on properties, foreclosures, real estate, and mortgages, among other topics. The Mortgage and Savings Center features
 the latest data on lending rates, and Money 101 is a guide on how to
 finance and purchase a home. Calculators compare the cost of living in
 regions throughout the United States, measure the average cost of home
 renovations, find the best mortgage rates, and determine affordable
 prices for individual budgets.

Fannie Mae (Foreclosure Prevention and Mortgage Assistance) (http://
 www.fanniemae.com/kb/index?page=home).
 Fannie Mae is "a government-sponsored enterprise (GSE) chartered by
 Congress with a mission to provide liquidity, stability and affordability
 to the U.S. housing and mortgage markets" (website). For home buyers
 and home owners, it provides practical advice on buying and owning a
 home and features a glossary of terms, counseling services, warnings
 against scams, foreclosure prevention, and counseling services. Fannie
 Mae also offers assistance in looking for homes and finding lenders,
 appraisers, and housing counselors.

Federal Home Loan Banks (FHLB) (http://www.fhlbanks.com).
 "The 12 Federal Home Loan Banks are a system of regional banks from
 which local lending institutions everywhere in America borrow funds
 to finance housing, economic development, infrastructure and jobs"
 (website). These banks are located in Atlanta, Chicago, Cincinnati, Dallas,
 Des Moines, Indianapolis, New York, Pittsburgh, San Francisco, Seattle,
 and Topeka. Over 8,000 banks in the United States belong to the Federal
 Home Loan Bank System. FHLB issues financial data on advances

(secured loans), mortgage loans, and net investments and advances (as a percentage of total assets).

Federal Housing Finance Agency (FHFA) (http://www.fhfa.gov).

The regulator and conservator of Fannie Mae and Freddie Mac and the regulator of the 12 Federal Home Loan Banks. The FHFA website features data on mortgage rates, housing market indicators (with links to data from the Census Bureau, National Association of Home Builders, and U.S. Department of Housing and Urban Development), the FHFA House Price Index, a house price calculator (enabling consumers to calculate the value of their homes), a news center, research papers, and staff working papers.

Freddie Mac (Federal Home Loan Mortgage Corporation) (http://www.freddiemac.com).

Freddie Mac aims to "meet the needs of the mortgage market by making home ownership and rental housing more affordable; reduce the number of foreclosures; and help families keep their homes" (website). Features Primary Mortgage Market Survey, with data for 15- and 30-year mortgages; guides for those looking to buy a home; guides to avoiding foreclosure; a directory of mortgage products available; borrower success stories; online courses; and properties for sale.

Ginnie Mae (Government National Mortgage Association) (http://www.ginniemae.gov).

The stated goal is to "help make affordable housing a reality for millions of low-and moderate-income households across America by channeling global capital in to the nation's housing markets" (website). Features glossary of terms, loan estimate calculator, buy-versus-rent calculator, press releases, and statistics on monthly issuance and remaining principal balance reports, fiscal year issuance activity comparison, and historical issuance activity report.

Harvard University. Joint Center for Housing Studies (http://www.jchs.harvard.edu).

The Joint Center for Housing Studies "is Harvard University's center for information and research on housing in the United States. The Joint Center analyzes the dynamic relationships between housing markets and economic, demographic, and social trends, providing leaders in government, business, and the non-profit sector with the knowledge needed to develop effective policies and strategies" (website). Publishes downloadable studies of housing marketing, including *America's Rental Housing: The Key to A Balanced National Policy* and *State of the Nation's Housing 2010* in addition to research reports on the housing market.

Mergent Online (http://www.mergentonline.com).

Features industry reports for property development, construction, and heavy construction. Industry reports are grouped by regions: North America, Europe, Asia Pacific, and Latin America. For example, the report for North American property development industry covers the United States and Canada. Each report features a sector overview (current trends including prices of residential property); sector performance (performance of companies on stock exchanges, stock price trends, and so on); leading companies in the industry; news of mergers, acquisitions, and alliances; market trends and outlook; and key references (list of sources of data and their websites).

Mortgage Bankers Association (MBA) (http://www.mbaa.org/default.htm).
National association representing the real estate finance industry. Publisher of various resources, including *Mortgage Banking Terms: A Working Glossary, Commercial Real Estate Finance Basics, Practical Guide to FHA Lending, Secondary Mortgage Market Basics,* and *Handbook of Mortgage Lending.* Also features statistics in *MBA Monthly Forecasts* (a quarterly forecast of key economic and mortgage market indicators), *MBA Quarterly Origination Estimates* (a historical record of mortgage loan origination estimates), and *MBA Monthly Commentaries* (commentary on the current mortgage finance and economic climates and how these trends affect mortgage markets).

National Apartment Association (http://www.naahq.org/Pages/welcome.aspx).
Serves the needs of multifamily housing owners, managers, developers, and suppliers. Publishes guides to managers on issues such as lead paint regulations and bedbug prevention.

National Association of Home Builders (NAHB) (http://www.nahb.org/page.aspx/generic/sectionID=150).
Trade association serving the housing industry and the public at large. NAHB provides home building industry statistics using data from private and government data. Among statistics included are those on building materials: data and reports, construction statistics, home sale prices, financial and mortgage markets, and NAHB's 55 plus Market Index. Also publishes online periodical publications for members with some sample issues available to nonmembers. Among these publications are *NAHB Housing Data-FAQ, Housing Starts and Metro Forecasts for 2010–2011,* and *National Outlook: A Monthly U.S. Housing Overview.*

National Association of Realtors (http://www.realtor.org).
Trade association for Realtors features *Realtor Magazine,* an online periodical containing news reports, blogs, a reader poll, market updates (news on home sales and mortgage rates), technology news (e.g., how to maintain a website), and webinars. Provides the latest housing indicators, among which are existing home sales, existing home median price, housing starts, pending home sales, and new home sales. Association members can access special research reports for on local markets, state fiscal conditions and taxes, and state economic impact of housing.

Plunkett, Jack W. *Plunkett's Real Estate & Construction Almanac.* Houston: Plunkett Research Annual. Annual (http://www.plunkettresearch.com).
Covers trends in residential construction, commercial construction, real estate brokerage, property management, real estate investment, hotels, shopping centers, mortgages, office buildings, real estate investment trusts, and company profiles.

Realty Trac (http://www.realtytrac.com/home).
    Contains searchable database to locate local foreclosure real estate listings
    by area of the country and statistics on total foreclosures sold, new fore-
    closures, and average sale price per foreclosure plus the top five cities
    offering the most foreclosures. Also contains a foreclosure blog and Fore-
    closure 101 (a guide to purchasing foreclosures, a glossary, a foreclosure
    bookstore, and information on how to avoid foreclosure).

Standard & Poor's NetAdvantage (http://www.netadvantage.standardand
    poors.com).
    Select "Industry Surveys" and search for relevant reports on home building
    and REITS (real estate investment trusts). The Homebuilding Industry
    Reports contain current environment for the U.S. housing market (with
    statistics on housing starts and mortgage rates), monthly housing industry
    statistics, average selling prices for new homes, and Standard & Poor's
    Homebuilding Outlook. Also features comparative company analysis
    with statistics on revenues, net income, equity ratios, balance sheet ratios,
    profit ratios, and per-share data. The Industry References feature sources
    of statistics, among which are periodicals, trade associations, and
    government agencies. The REITS reports contain the current environment
    for investing, new private construction statistics, value of shopping mall
    construction, vacancy rates, rental apartments versus home ownership,
    comparative company analysis, and industry references, sources of statis-
    tics among which are periodicals, trade associations, and online resources.

United Nations Economic Commission for Europe Committee on Housing
    and Land Management (http://www.unece.org/hlm/welcome.html).
    The committee provides "a forum for the compilation, dissemination and
    exchange of information and experience on housing, urban development,
    land administration policies" (website). Features searchable database coun-
    try profiles on the housing sector in individual countries. The online reports
    for each country feature socioeconomic trends and housing policies, existing
    housing stock and new construction, housing finance, land administration,
    and spatial planning and recommendations by the committee.

U.S. Census Bureau. Economic Indicators (http://www.census.gov/cgi-bin/
    briefroom/BriefRm).
    Among the economic indicators listed are statistics for construction spend-
    ing, new home sales, housing starts/building permits, and housing vacan-
    cies and home ownership. "Construction Spending" features current data
    and archived data for 1993 to the present and 1964–2001. Data issued per
    month contains total spending for the month, private construction spend-
    ing, public construction spending, value of construction put in the United
    States for the past several months, and coefficients of variation and stan-
    dard errors by type of construction. Chart is also available for construction
    expenditures, seasonally adjusted annual rate. "New Home Sales" pro-
    vides data on sales of new one family homes with a chart and current
    and archived data. Each month's release contains statistics for new houses
    sold and for sale, homes sold by sale price, and new homes sold by stage of

construction and median number of months on sales market. "Housing Starts/Building Permits" features current monthly data and archived releases and historic time series (1959 to the present) plus a monthly chart. Each monthly release contains data for privately owned housing units authorized by building permits, housing starts, housing completions, statistical tables for new privately owned housing units issued by permit-issuing places, and new privately owned housing units authorized but not started at end of period. "Housing Vacancies and Home Ownership" data issued on a quarterly basis provides statistics for home ownership rate, rental vacancy rate, and home owner vacancy rate (by percentages with analysis of regions of the United States). Archived releases (1994 to the present) and historic time series (1956 to the present). Each quarterly report contains detailed tables for vacancy rates for the United States, 1960 and 1965–2009; vacancy rates by area; estimates of the housing inventory; home ownership rates for the United States, 1965–2009; home owner-ship rates by age of householder; characteristics of vacant units by region; and characteristics of vacant units by units in structure.

U.S. Census Bureau. Industry Reports Series. Construction
(http://www.census.gov/econ/census02/guide/INDRPT23.HTM).
Data for 2002 Economic Census on Construction includes construction of buildings (e.g., new single-family construction and new multifamily housing construction), heavy and civil engineering construction (e.g., land subdivision); and specialty trade contractors (e.g., masonry and siding contractors). The scope of the Construction sector report is as follows: "The Construction sector (sector 23) comprises establishments primarily engaged in the construction of buildings or engineering projects (e.g. highways and utility systems). Establishments primarily engaged in the preparation of sites for new construction and establishments primarily engaged in subdividing land for sale, as building sites also are included in this sector. Construction work done may include new work, additions, alterations, or maintenance and repairs. Activities of these establishments generally are managed at a fixed place of business, but they usually perform construction activities at multiple project sites. Production responsibilities for establishments in this sector are usually specified in (1) contracts with the owners of construction projects (prime contracts) or (2) contracts with other construction establishments (subcontracts)." Statistical data and report information for Construction ranges from general construction of building for data on drywall and insulation contractors, siding contractors, roofing contractors, and electrical contractors. Each listed component (e.g., New Housing Operative Builders) opens to a Full Report in PDF and also to a table in PDF. Each Full Report includes an explanation of the 2002 Census then opens to detailed tables related to the specific component of the Economic Census on Construction. Please note that 2007 Census information may be found on the link (as shown on the following sample) to American FactFinder. Also, the U.S. Census Bureau makes it possible to order paper copies through custom print format.

2002 Economic Census
Industry Series
Reports
Construction

2007 Economic Census data are available in American FactFinder. See also the current Industry Statistics Sampler.

You are here: 2002 Economic Census ▶ Guide ▶ Schedule ▶ Industry Series ▶ **Construction**

Industry Series data are preliminary and are subject to change; they will be superseded by data released in later reports.

All of these data are available in American FactFinder in a form that can be manipulated. Data are released on DVD-ROM quarterly starting in early 2005 and may lag availability in PDF by up to four months. Paper copies of these reports can be purchased through the custom print service.

NAICS code	Report title	Report number	Projected or actual release (PDF)	Full report Link to PDF	Size in kb	Tables only Link to PDF	Size in kb
236	**Construction of Buildings**						
236115	New Single-Family Housing Construction (except Operative Builders)	EC02-23I-236115(RV)	07/22/2005	[PDF]	455	[PDF]	241
236116	New Multifamily Housing Construction (except Operative Builders)	EC02-23I-236116	01/07/2005	[PDF]	437	[PDF]	223
236117	New Housing Operative Builders	EC02-23I-236117(RV)	07/22/2005	[PDF]	454	[PDF]	240
236118	Residential Remodelers	EC02-23I-236118(RV)	11/21/2005	[PDF]	454	[PDF]	238
236210	Industrial Building Construction	EC02-23I-236210	01/07/2005	[PDF]	437	[PDF]	223
236220	Commercial and Institutional Building Construction	EC02-23I-236220	12/30/2004	[PDF]	442	[PDF]	228
237	**Heavy and Civil Engineering Construction**						
237110	Water and Sewer Line and Related Structures Construction	EC02-23I-237110	01/07/2005	[PDF]	444	[PDF]	229
237120	Oil and Gas Pipeline and Related Structures Construction	EC02-23I-237120	01/10/2005	[PDF]	437	[PDF]	223
237130	Power and Communication Line and Related Structures Construction	EC02-23I-237130	12/29/2004	[PDF]	440	[PDF]	225
237210	Land Subdivision	EC02-23I-237210	12/30/2004	[PDF]	438	[PDF]	223
237310	Highway, Street, and Bridge Construction	EC02-23I-237310	12/30/2004	[PDF]	440	[PDF]	226
237990	Other Heavy and Civil Engineering Construction	EC02-23I-237990	01/07/2005	[PDF]	441	[PDF]	227
238	**Specialty Trade Contractors**						
238110	Poured Concrete Foundation and Structure Contractors	EC02-23I-238110	12/29/2004	[PDF]	441	[PDF]	226
238120	Structural Steel and Precast Concrete Contractors	EC02-23I-238120	12/29/2004	[PDF]	439	[PDF]	225
238130	Framing Contractors	EC02-23I-238130	12/29/2004	[PDF]	439	[PDF]	224
238140	Masonry Contractors	EC02-23I-238140	12/29/2004	[PDF]	442	[PDF]	228
238150	Glass and Glazing Contractors	EC02-23I-238150	12/30/2004	[PDF]	437	[PDF]	223
238160	Roofing Contractors	EC02-23I-238160	12/29/2004	[PDF]	439	[PDF]	225
238170	Siding Contractors	EC02-23I-238170	12/30/2004	[PDF]	439	[PDF]	224
238190	Other Foundation, Structure, and Building Exterior Contractors	EC02-23I-238190	01/06/2005	[PDF]	441	[PDF]	227
238210	Electrical Contractors	EC02-23I-238210	12/29/2004	[PDF]	444	[PDF]	230
238220	Plumbing, Heating, and Air-Conditioning Contractors	EC02-23I-238220	12/30/2004	[PDF]	446	[PDF]	232
238290	Other Building Equipment Contractors	EC02-23I-238290	01/07/2005	[PDF]	439	[PDF]	225
238310	Drywall and Insulation Contractors	EC02-23I-238310	12/29/2004	[PDF]	441	[PDF]	227
238320	Painting and Wall Covering Contractors	EC02-23I-238320	12/29/2004	[PDF]	443	[PDF]	229
238330	Flooring Contractors	EC02-23I-238330	12/30/2004	[PDF]	439	[PDF]	225
238340	Tile and Terrazzo Contractors	EC02-23I-238340	12/30/2004	[PDF]	439	[PDF]	225
238350	Finish Carpentry Contractors	EC02-23I-238350	12/29/2004	[PDF]	439	[PDF]	225
238390	Other Building Finishing Contractors	EC02-23I-238390	01/06/2005	[PDF]	438	[PDF]	224
238910	Site Preparation Contractors	EC02-23I-238910	12/29/2004	[PDF]	448	[PDF]	233
238990	All Other Specialty Trade Contractors	EC02-23I-238990	01/06/2005	[PDF]	448	[PDF]	234

Source: U.S. Census Bureau, 2002 Economic Census

U.S. Department of Housing and Urban Development (HUD)
 (http://portal.hud.gov/portal/page/portal/HUD).
 HUD's mission statement is "to create strong, sustainable, inclusive communities and quality affordable homes for all. HUD is working to
 strengthen the housing market to bolster the economy and protect consumers; meet the need for quality affordable rental homes; utilize housing as a platform for improving quality of life; build inclusive and
 sustainable communities free from discrimination; and transform the
 way HUD does business" (website). Provides databases for affordable
 apartment searches, HUD homes available for purchase nationwide,
 buy-versus-rent calculators, a home ownership mortgage calculator, and
 HUD-approved housing counselor agencies. Accessible also are official
 forms, an FHA Mortgage Starter Kit, a glossary of terms, and forms for
 housing discrimination complaints, among other forms and publications.
 Features links to states; for instance, HUD in New York provides local
 resources, including HUD homes for sale and filing a housing discrimination complaint. The Federal Housing Administration (FHA), a part of
 HUD, is the largest government insurer of mortgages in the world and
 mortgage insurance on single-family, multifamily, and manufactured
 homes and hospital loans made by FHA-approved lenders throughout
 the United States

Urban Land Institute (http://www.uli.org).
 Institute for community builders, that is, those who develop and redevelop
 neighborhoods, business districts in the United States and internationally. Publisher of *Urban Land Online Magazine*, *Emerging Trends in Real Estate*,
 Refitting Office Buildings to Be Green and Energy Efficient, and *Real Estate Market Analysis*. Features the online member resource Real Estate Barometer,
 which helps track and understand key economic and financial trends
 affecting the real estate business. Covers all aspects of real estate, among
 which are real estate capital markets, commercial/multifamily investment,
 and property and housing. The most recent Real Estate Barometer is found
 in the "Capital Markets" section of *Urban Land Online Magazine*.

ONLINE DATABASES AND PERIODICAL ACCESS

Databases to search for articles on real estate include *ABI/INFORM*,
Business Source Premier and *ScienceDirect*.

PERIODICALS AND NEWSPAPERS

Builder (http://www.builderonline.com)
Commercial Investment Real Estate (http://www.ciremagazine.com)
Commercial Property News (http://www.cpnonline.com)
Journal of Housing Economics (http://www.elsevier.com/wps/find/
 journaldescription.cws_home/622881/description#description)

Journal of Property Management (https://www.irem.org/sechome.cfm
    ?sec=jpm)
Journal of Real Estate Literature (http://cbeweb-1.fullerton.edu/finance/jrel)
Journal of Real Estate Portfolio Management (http://cbeweb-1.fullerton.edu/
    finance/jrepm)
Multi-Housing News (http://www.multi-housingnews.com)
National Real Estate Investor (http://nreionline.com)
Real Estate Finance (http://www.aspenpublishers.com/product.asp?catalog
    _name=Aspen&product_id=SS0748318X&cookie%5Ftest=1)
Real Estate Law Journal (http://west.thomson.com/productdetail/4169/
    14938682/productdetail.aspx)

Appendix I

Acronyms and Abbreviations

AA	Affirmative Action
AACSB	American Assembly of Collegiate Schools of Business
ABA	American Bankers Association
ABA	American Bar Association
ABU	Abstracted Business Information
Acctg	Accounting
ACH	Automated Clearing House
ADB	Asian Development Bank
Adm	Administration
ADR	American Depository Receipts
AICPA	American Institute of Certified Public Accountants
AMA	American Management Association
AMA	American Management Association
AMEX	American Stock Exchange
APB	Accounting Principles Board
APR	Annual Percentage Rate
APY	Annual Percentage Yield
ARBA	*American Reference Books Annual*
ARF	Advertising Research Foundation
ARM	Adjustable-Rate Mortgage
ARR	Average Rate of Return
ARS	Annual Report to Shareholders
ASAP	As Soon As Possible
ASB	Auditing Standards Board (AICPA)
ASI	*American Statistics Index*
ATM	Automatic Teller Machine
BBB	Better Business Bureau

(*continued*)

BEA	Bureau of Economic Analysis
BIS	Bank for International Settlements
BOP	Balance of Payments
BOT	Balance of Trade
BOT	Board of Trustees
BPI	*Business Periodicals Index*
BRASS	Business Reference and Services Section, American Library Association
BSE	Boston Stock Exchange
CBOE	Chicago Board Options Exchange
CBOT	Chicago Board of Trade
CCH	Commerce Clearing House
CD	Certificate of Deposit
CEA	Council of Economic Advisers
CEO	Chief Executive Officer
CFA	Chartered Financial Analyst
CFO	Chief Financial Officer
CFP	Certified Financial Planner
CFTC	Commodities Futures Trading Commission
ChBd	Chairman of the Board
CHX	Chicago Stock Exchange
CIO	Chief Information Officer
CIS	Congressional Information Service, Inc.
CME	Chicago Mercantile Exchange
CMO	Chief Marketing Officer
Co.	Company
COB	Close of Business
COBRA	Consolidated Budget Reconciliation Act
COD	Cash on Delivery
COLA	Cost-of-Living Adjustment
CPA	Certified Public Accountant
CPI	Consumer Price Index
CRB	Commodity Research Bureau
CSCE	Coffee, Sugar, and Cocoa Exchange
CUSIP	Committee on Uniform Securities Identification Procedures
DA	Deposit Account
D & B	Dun & Bradstreet
DJI	Dow Jones Index
DJIA	Dow Jones Industrial Average

DJTA	Dow Jones Transportation Average
DJUA	Dow Jones Utility Average
DOC	Department of Commerce
DOL	Department of Labor
DOT	Department of The Treasury
DRIP	Dividend Reinvestment Plan
D-U-N-S	Dun's Universal Numbering System (Dun & Bradstreet)
EC	European Community
ECB	European Central Bank
ECE	Economic Commission for Europe
ECOA	Equal Credit Opportunity Act
EDGAR	Electronic Data Gathering, Analysis and Retrieval (SEC)
EDR	European Depository Receipt
EEC	European Economic Community
EEOC	Equal Employment Opportunity Commission
EESA	Emergency Economic Stabilization Act of 2008
EFT	Electronic Funds Transfer
EITF	Emerging Issues Task Force
EOM	End of Month
EPA	Environmental Protection Agency
EPR	Earnings Price Ratio
EPS	Earnings Per Share
ETF	Exchange Traded Fund
ESOP	Employee Stock Ownership Plan
EU	European Union
EXIMBANK	Export Import Bank
FAQ	Frequently Asked Questions
FASB	Financial Accounting Standards Board
FCC	Federal Communications Commission
FDA	Food and Drug Administration
FDI	Federal Direct Investment
FDIC	Federal Deposit Insurance Corporation
Fed	Federal Reserve System
FET	Federal Excise Tax
FHA	Federal Housing Administration
FHFB	Federal Housing Finance Board
FHLB	Federal Home Loan Bank

(continued)

FHLBB	Federal Home Loan Bank Board
FHLBS	Federal Home Loan Bank System
FHLMC	Federal Home Loan Mortgage Corporation (Freddie Mac)
FICA	Federal Insurance Contributions Act
FIFO	First In, First Out
FIT	Federal Income Tax
FIN	Federal ID Number
FNMA	Federal National Mortgage Association (Fannie Mae)
FOC	Free of Charge
FOMC	Federal Open Market Committee (Federal Reserve System)
FRA	Federal Reserve Act
FRB	Federal Reserve Board
Freddie Mac	Federal Home Loan Mortgage Corporation
FRM	Fixed Rate Mortgage
FRS	Federal Reserve System
FSLIC	Federal Savings and Loan Corporation
FTC	Federal Trade Commission
FTE	Full-Time Equivalent
FY	Fiscal Year
FYA	For Your Attention
FYI	For Your Information
GAAP	Generally Accepted Accounting Principles
GAO	General Accounting Office
GASB	Governmental Accounting Standards Board
GATT	General Agreement on Tariffs and Trade
GC	General Counsel
GDP	Gross Domestic Product
GDR	Global Depository Receipt
G-8	Group of Eight Finance Ministers
Ginnie Mae	Government National Mortgage Association
GM	General Manager
GMC	Guaranteed Mortgage Certificate
GNMA	Government National Mortgage Association (Ginnie Mae)
GNP	Gross National Product
GPO	Government Printing Office
GSA	General Services Administration
HELOC	Home Equity Line of Credit

HMI	Housing Market Index
HMO	Health Maintenance Organization
HQ	Headquarters
HR	House of Representatives
HR	Human Resources
HUD	Department of Housing and Urban Development
IBRD	International Bank for Reconstruction and Development (World Bank)
ICC	International Chamber of Commerce
ICC	Interstate Commerce Commission
ICFP	Institute of Certified Financial Planners
ILO	International Labor Organization
IMF	International Monetary Fund
Inc.	Incorporated
IOU	I Owe You
IPO	Initial Public Offering
IR	Investor Relations
IRA	Individual Retirement Account
IRC	Internal Revenue Code
IRS	Internal Revenue Service
ISE	International Securities Exchange
ITA	International Trade Association
JA	Joint Account
JIT	Just-in-Time (Management)
KCBT	Kansas City Board of Trade
LDC	Less Developed Country
L/I	Letter of Intent
LIFO	Last In First Out
LLC	Limited Liability Company
LMRA	Labor-Management Relations Act
LSE	London Stock Exchange
Ltd	Limited (British Corporation)
MBA	Master of Business Administration
MBA	Mortgage Bankers of America
MBO	Management Buyout
MBO	Management by Objective
MERC	Chicago Mercantile Exchange
MGE	Minneapolis Grain Exchange
MIS	Management Information System

(continued)

MSI	Marketing Science Institute
MSRP	Manufacturer's Suggested Retail Price
MUNI	Municipal Security
NAFTA	North American Free Trade Agreement
NAHB	National Association of Home Builders
NAIC	National Association of Insurance Commissioners
NAICS	North American Industry Classification System
NAR	National Association of Realtors
NAREIT	National Association of Real Estate Investment Trusts
NASAA	North American Securities Administrators Association
NASD	National Association of Securities Dealers
NASDAQ	National Association of Securities Dealers Automated Quotation
NAV	Net Asset Value
NBER	National Bureau of Economic Research
NCV	No Commercial Value
NFA	National Futures Association
NFCC	National Foundation for Credit Counseling
NL	No Load
NLRA	National Labor Relations Act
NMS	National Market System
NOI	Net Operating Income
NOL	Net Operating Loss
NP	Notary Public
NPV	Net Present Value
NPV	No Par Value
NQB	National Quotation Bureau
NR	Not Rated
NSCC	National Securities Clearing Association
NSF	Not Sufficient Funds (Banking)
NYFE	New York Futures Exchange
NYMEX	New York Mercantile Exchange
NYSE	New York Stock Exchange
OD	Overdraft, Overdrawn
OECD	Organization for Economic Cooperation and Development
OMB	Office of Management and Budget
OOH	*Occupational Outlook Handbook*
OPEC	Organization of Petroleum Exporting Countries

OSHA	Occupational Safety and Health Act of 1970
OSHA	Occupational Safety and Health Administration
O/T	Overtime
OTC	Over the Counter
P	Put (in Options Listings)
PA	Public Accountant
P&L	Profit and Loss Statement
P/E	Price-Earnings Ratio
PFD	Preferred Stock
PHLX	Philadelphia Stock Exchange
PIN	Personal Identification Number
PN	Promissory Note
POP	Point of Purchase
PPI	Producer Price Index
PR	Public Relations
Prop	Proprietor
PT	Part-Time
PV	Present Value
QA	Quality Assurance
QC	Quality Control
R&D	Research and Development
REIT	Real Estate Investment Trust
ROA	Return on Assets
ROC	Return on Capital
ROE	Return on Equity
ROI	Return on Investment
S&L	Savings and Loan
S&P	Standard & Poor's Corporation
Sallie Mae	Student Loan Marketing Association (SLM Corp.)
SB	Savings Bond
SBA	Small Business Administration
SBIC	Small Business Investment Corporation
SBLI	Savings Bank Life Insurance
SCORE	Service Corps of Retired Executives
SDB	Special District Bond
SDRs	Special Drawing Rights
SE	Shareholders' Equity
SEC	Securities and Exchange Commission
SF	Sinking Fund

(continued)

SIC	Standard Industrial Classification
SLA	Special Libraries Association
SLMA	Student Loan Marketing Association (Sallie Mae)
SMSA	Standard Metropolitan Statistical Area
SOP	Standard Operating Procedure
SPX	Standard & Poor's 500 Stock Index
SRDS	Standard Rate and Data Service
SRI	*Statistical Reference Index*
SS	Social Security
SSA	Social Security Administration
SUDOCS	Superintendent of Documents
T BILL	Treasury Bill
TBA	To Be Announced
TC	Tax Court of the United States
TCO	Total Cost of Ownership
TM	Trade Mark
TQM	Total Quality Management
Trst	Trustee
TSR	Total Shareholder Return
USC	United States Code
USDA	United States Department of Agriculture
VAT	Value-Added Tax
VC	Venture Capital
Veep	Vice President
VL	*Value Line Investment Survey*
VP	Vice President
WSJ	*Wall Street Journal*
W/Tax	Withholding Tax
WTO	World Trade Organization
YLD	Yield (in Stock Listings)
ZBB	Zero-Based Budgeting
ZR	Zero Coupon Issue

Appendix II

Major Business Libraries

Babson College
Horn Library
Babson Park, MA 02457
781-239-4596
http://www3.babson.edu/library

Boston Public Library
Kirsten Business Library
700 Boylston Street
Boston, MA 02116
617-859-2142
http://www.bpl.org/research/kbb/kbbhome.htm

Boston University Library
Frederick S. Pardee Management Library
595 Commonwealth Avenue
Boston, MA 02215
Reference: 617-353-4303
http://www.bu.edu/library/management/index.shtml

Brooklyn Public Library
Business Library
Brooklyn Heights Library
280 Cadman Plaza West at Tillary Street
Brooklyn, NY 11201
718-623-7100
http://www.brooklynpubliclibrary.org/business

Columbia University Libraries
Thomas J. Watson Library of Business and Economics
130 Unis Hall
3022 Broadway
New York, NY 10027
212-854-7804
http://library.columbia.edu/indiv/business.html

Cornell University
Johnson Graduate School of Management
Management Library
101 Sage Hall
Ithaca, NY 14853
607-255-3389
http://johnson.library.cornell.edu

Dartmouth College Library
Feldberg Business and Engineering Library
Dartmouth College Library
Hanover, NH 03755
603-646-2560
http://www.dartmouth.edu/~feldberg/common/index.php

Duke University
The Fuqua School of Business
Ford Library
Box 90120
Duke University
Durham, NC 27708-0120
919-660-3795
http://library.fuqua.duke.edu

Emory Libraries
Goizueta Business Library
Robert W. Woodruff Library
540 Asbury Circle
Atlanta, GA 30322
404-727-1641
http://business.library.emory.edu

Harvard University Business School
Baker Library/Bloomberg Center
Soldiers Field

Boston, MA 02163
617-495-6040
http://www.library.hbs.edu

Indiana University Libraries
Business/SPEA Information Commons
SPEA 150
1315 East Tenth Street
Bloomington, IN 47405
812-855-1957
http://www.libraries.iub.edu/index.php?pageId=77

James J. Hill Reference Library
80 West Fourth Street
St. Paul, MN 55102
877-700-HILL (4455); local: 651-5500
http://www.jjhill.org

Library of Congress
Business Reference Services
(Science, Technology and Business Division)
101 Independence Ave SE
Washington, DC 20540
202-707-5000
http://www.loc.gov/rr/business

Long Island University
C. W. Post Campus
B. Davis Schwartz Memorial Library
Center for Business Research
720 Northern Boulevard
Brookville, NY 11548
516-299-2832
http://www2.liu.edu/cwis/cwp/library/cbr/
cbrhome.htm

Massachusetts Institute of Technology
Dewey Library
30 Wadsworth Street
Cambridge, MA 02139
617-253-5676
http://info-libraries.mit.edu/dewey/

New York Public Library
Science, Industry and Business Library
188 Madison Avenue at 34th Street
New York, NY 10016
212-275-6975
http://www.nypl.org/locations/sibl

New York University Libraries
Virtual Business Library
Elmer Holmes Bobst Library
70 Washington Square South
New York, NY 10012
212-998-2500
http://library.nyu.edu/vbl

Ohio State University
Fisher College of Business
Thompson Library
Library Resources for Business
1858 Neil Avenue Mall
Columbus, OH 43210
614-292-OSUL
http://fisher.osu.edu/library-resources

Princeton University
Industrial Relations Library
Firestone Library
One Washington Road
Princeton, NJ 08544
609-258-4043
http://libguides.princeton.edu/industrel

Princeton University
Pliny Fisk Library of Economics and Finance
Firestone Library
One Washington Road
Princeton, NJ 08544
609-258-3211
http://firestone.princeton.edu/econlib

Purdue University
Management and Economics Library
Krannert Building

Second Floor
403 West State Street
West Lafayette, IN 47907-2056
765-494-2920
http://www.lib.purdue.edu/mel

Rutgers, The State University of New Jersey
John Cotton Dana Library
185 University Avenue
Newark, NJ 07102-1814
973-353-5901
http://www.libraries.rutgers.edu/rul/libs/dana_lib/dana_lib.shtml

St. John's University
School of Risk Management
The Kathryn and Sheldon Cullum Davis Library
101 Murray Street
Third Floor
New York, NY 10007
212-277-5135
http://www.stjohns.edu/academics/libraries/campus/davis

Stanford University Graduate School of Business
J. Hugh Jackson Library
518 Memorial Way
Stanford, CA 94305-5016
650-723-2162
http://www.gsb.stanford.edu/jacksonlibrary

University of California, Berkeley
Thomas J. Long Business Library
Haas School of Business
S3250
2220 Piedmont Avenue
Berkeley, CA 94720
510-642-0400
http://www.lib.berkeley.edu/BUSI

University of California, Los Angeles
Anderson School of Management
Rosenfeld Library
110 Westwood Plaza
E-301

Box 951460
Los Angeles, CA 90095-1460
310-825-3138
http://www.anderson.ucla.edu/library.xml

University of Cincinnati Libraries
UC Internet Business and Economics Library
PO Box 210033
Cincinnati, OH 45221
513-536-1424
http://libraries.uc.edu/research/subject_resources/business

University of Illinois at Urbana-Champaign
Business and Economics Library
1408 West Gregory Drive
Urbana, IL 61801
217-333-2290
http://www.library.illinois.edu/bel

University of Michigan Ross School of Business
Kresge Business Administration Library
701 Tappan
Room K3330
Ann Arbor, MI 48109
734-764-9464
http://www.bus.umich.edu/KresgeLibrary

University of Pennsylvania
The Wharton School
Lippincott Library
3420 Walnut Street
Philadelphia, PA 19104
215-898-5924
http://www.library.upenn.edu/lippincott

University of Pittsburgh
Business Library
University of Pittsburgh
118 Mervis Hall
Pittsburgh, PA 15260
412-648-1669
http://www.library.pitt.edu/libraries/business/business.html

University of Rochester
River Campus Libraries
755 Library Road
PO Box 270055
Rochester, NY 14627
585-275-4478
http://www.library.rochester.edu/bgil/home

University of Washington
University Libraries
Foster Business Library
Foster Business Library
Box 353224
Seattle, WA 98195
206-543-4360
http://www.lib.washington.edu/business

University of Wisconsin–Madison
Business Library
2200 Grainger Hall
975 University Avenue
Madison, WI 53706
608-265-6202
http://business.library.wisc.edu/index.html

Villanova University
Falvey Memorial Library
Bartley Business Information Center
800 East Lancaster Avenue
Villanova, PA 19085
610-519-4270
http://library.villanova.edu/about/librariesandcollections/vbl

World Bank and IMF Libraries
Joint Bank Fund Library
700 19th Street NW
Room IMF C-700
Washington, DC 20431
202-623-7054
http://external.worldbankimflib.org/external.htm

Appendix III

Directory of Major Business-Related Federal Government Departments, Agencies, and Resources

Name	URL	Description
Consumer Product Safety Commission	http://cpsc.gov	Responsible for ensuring safety of consumer products, develops safety standards, and promotes research; alerts consumers to product problems and hazards
Economic Report of the President	http:// www.gpoaccess.gov/ eop	Focuses on the economic year in review with projections for the future
Equal Employment Opportunity Commission	http://www.eeoc.gov	Oversees compliance and enforcement activities for equal employment opportunities in the workplace; features litigation statistics and manuals and guides
Federal Deposit Insurance Corporation	http://www.fdic.gov	Independent agency created by Congress that aims to stability and public confidence in nation's financial system; publishes statistics on banking

(continued)

Federal Reserve System	http://www.federalreserve.gov	Oversees monetary policy and supervises and regulates the nation's banks; source of data on U.S. banking statistics
Internal Revenue Service	http://www.irs.gov	Administers tax collection and provides online form and statistics
National Labor Relations Board	http://www.nlrb.gov	Safeguards employees rights to organize and have unions as bargaining representatives; features information on laws and regulations and guides
Census Bureau	http://www.census.gov	Source of data about the nation's people and economy; features current at retrospective data on population and the economy
Commodity Futures Trading Commission	http://www.cftc.gov	Created by Congress as an independent agency to regulate commodity futures and options markets in the United States
Department of Agriculture	http://www.usda.gov	Provides agricultural statistics for livestock, plants, animals
Department of Commerce, Bureau of Economic Analysis	http://www.bea.gov	Source of economic statistics; publisher of *Survey of Current Business*
Department of Commerce, Economics and Statistics Administration	http://www.economicindicators.gov	Links to economic data including gross domestic product, personal income and outlays, construction, and so on
Department of Commerce, International Trade Commission	http://www.trade.gov	Provides annual and quarterly trade data
Department of Housing and Urban Development	http://www.hud.gov/	Aims to create strong communities and provide affordable homes; provides information sources forms, and database of homes available for purchase

Department of Labor, Bureau of Labor Statistics	http://www.bls.gov	Contains economic news releases and data on employment and unemployment, productivity, workplace injuries, and so on
Department of the Treasury	http://www.ustreas.gov	Manages federal finances, currency, and tax collection; publisher of the *Treasury Bulletin*
Federal Communications Commission	http://www.fcc.gov	Regulates interstate and international communications by radio, television, and so on
Federal Trade Commission	http://www.ftc.gov/index.shtml	Provides competition jurisdiction and consumer protection
Food and Drug Administration	http://www.fda.gov	Provides product information and consumer safety alerts
Mint	http://www.usmint.gov	Produces coinage for the United States; contains statistical data in its annual reports
Securities and Exchange Commission	http://www.sec.gov	Securities market regulatory agency; contains EDGAR, a repository of public company reports including, 10K and 10Q
Small Business Association	http://www.sba.gov	Provides assistance, counseling and advice to small-business owners; publisher of e-newsletter, start-up guides, and so on
Social Security Administration	http://www.ssa.gov	Features data about Social Security, Medicare, and so on

Appendix IV

Major Stock Markets and Securities Exchanges

ARGENTINA
Buenos Aires Stock Exchange (http://www.bcba.sba.com.ar/home/index.php)

AUSTRALIA
Asian Pacific Exchange Limited (http://www.apx.com.au/APX/EN/Default.aspx)
Australian Securities Exchange (http://www.asx.com.au/)

AUSTRIA
Wiener Boerse (http://www.wienerborse.at/)

BAHRAIN
Bahrain Bourse (http://www.bahrainbourse.com.bh/bb)

BOTSWANA
Botswana Stock Exchange (http://www.bse.co.bw/)

BRAZIL
BM&FBOVESPA (http://www.bmfbovespa.com.br)

CANADA
Canadian National Stock Exchange (http://www.cng.ca/)
Montreal Exchange (http://www.m-x.ca/accueil_en.php)
NASDAQ Canada (http://www.nasdaq-canada.com/asp/nasdaq Canada.asp?language=E)
TMX Group (http://www.tmx.com/)
Toronto Stock Exchange (http://www.tmx.com/)

CAYMAN ISLANDS
Cayman Islands Stock Exchange (http://www.csx.com.ky/)

CHILE
Santiago Stock Exchange
(http://www.bolsadesantiago.com)

CHINA
Shanghai Stock Exchange (http://www.sse.com.cn/sseportal/en/
home/home.shtml)
Shenzhen Stock Exchange (http://www.szse.cn/main/en/)

COLOMBIA
Bolsa de Valores de Colombia (BVC)
(http://www.bvc.com.co/pps/tibco/portalbvc)

CZECH REPUBLIC
Prague Stock Exchange (http://www.pse.cz/)

DOMINICAN REPUBLIC
Bolsa de Valores de la República Dominicana (BVRD) (http://
www.bolsard.com/app/do/frontpage.aspx)

EASTERN CARIBBEAN
Eastern Caribbean Securities Exchange (http://www.ecseonline.com/)

EGYPT
Egyptian Exchange
(http://egyptse.com/english/homepage.aspx)

EUROPE
Euronext (http://www.euronext.com)

FIJI
South Pacific Stock Exchange (http://www.spse.com.fj/)

GERMANY
Deutsch Boerse(http://deutsche-boerse.com/dbag/dispatch/en/
kir/gdb_navigation/home)

GHANA
Ghana Stock Exchange (http://www.gse.com.gh/)

GREECE
Athens Stock Exchange (http://www.ase.gr/default_en.asp)

GUATEMALA
Bolsa Nacional de Valores (BNV)
(http://www.bvnsa.com.gt/bvnsa/index.php)

HONG KONG
Hong Kong Exchanges and Cleaning Limited (http://www.hkex.com.hk
/eng/index.htm)

HUNGARY
Budapest Stock Exchange (http://www.bse.hu/)

INDIA
Bombay Stock Exchange (http://www.bseindia.com/)
National Stock Exchange of India (http://www.nseindia.com/)

INDONESIA
Indonesia Stock Exchange
(http://www.idx.co.id/)

IRAN
Tehran Stock Exchange (http://www.iranbourse.com/default.aspx?
tabid=36)

IRAQ
Iraq Stock Exchange (http://www.isx-iq.net/isxportal/portal/
homePage.html?currlanguage=en)

IRELAND
Irish Stock Exchange (http://www.ise.ie/)

ISRAEL
Tel Aviv Stock Exchange (http://www.tase.co.il/taseens/
homepage.htm)

JAMAICA
Jamaica Stock Exchange (http://www.jamstockex.com/)

JAPAN
Tokyo Stock Exchange (http://www.tse.or.jp/english)

SPAIN
BME Spanish Exchanges (http://www.bolsasymercados.es/
ing.home.html)

NEW ZEALAND
New Zealand Exchange
(http://www.nzx.com/home)

PAKISTAN
Karachi Stock Exchange (http://www.kse.com.pk/)

PALESTINE
Palestine Exchange (http://www.pex.ps/PSEWebSite/Entrance.aspx)

PHILIPPINES
Philippine Stock Exchange (http://www.pse.com.ph/)

POLAND
Warsaw Stock Exchange (http://www.gpw.pl/)

RUSSIA
RTS Stock Exchange (http://www.rts.ru/)
St. Petersburg Stock Exchange (http://www.spbex.ru/)

SOUTH KOREA
Korea Exchange (http://www.krx.co.kr/index.jsp)

SWITZERLAND
SIX Swiss Exchange (http://www.six-swiss-exchange.com/index
_de.html)

SYRIA
Damascus Securities Exchange (http://www.dse.sy/)

TURKEY
Istanbul Stock Exchange (http://www.ise.org/Home.aspx)

UGANDA
Uganda Securities Exchange (http://www.use.or.ug/)

UNITED ARAB EMIRATES
Abu Dhabi Securities Exchange (http://www.adx.ae/English/Pages/
default.aspx)
Dubai Financial Market (http://www.dfm.ae/Default.aspx)

UNITED KINGDOM
London Stock Exchange (http://www.londonstockexchange.com/
home/homepage.htm)
PLUS Stock Exchange (http://www.plus-sx.com/home.html;jsessio-
nid=956B39A8AE962310B2B8A75DA6260FB3)

UNITED STATES

American Stock Exchange (AMEX) (http://www.nyse.com/attachment/amex_landing.htm)

BATS (Better Alternative Trading System) Exchange (http://www.batstrading.com/)

Boston Stock Exchange (http://www.nasdaqtrader.com/Trader.aspx?id=Boston_Stock_Exchange). Acquired by NASDAQ OMX

Chicago Board Options Exchange (CBOE) (http://www.cboe.com/)

Chicago Stock Exchange (CHX) (http://www.chx.com/)

Direct Edge

(http://www.directedge.com/)

International Securities Exchange

(http://www.ise.com/)

NASDAQ (http://www.nasdaq.com/)

National Stock Exchange (http://www.nsx.com/)

New York Stock Exchange (http://www.nyse.com/)

VENEZUELA

Bolsa de Valores de Caracas (BVC) (http://www.caracasstock.com/)

ZIMBABWE

Zimbabwe Stock Exchange (http://www.zse.co.zw/)

Index

About the Author

LUCY HECKMAN is associate professor and head of the Reference Department at the St. John's University Library, Queens, NY. Her published works include *The New York Stock Exchange: A Guide to Information Sources*, *NASDAQ: A Guide to Information Sources*, *Franchising in Business: A Guide to Information Sources*, and *Damascus*.